London, Brighton & South Coast Railway Album

London, Brighton & South Coast Railway Album

Klaus Marx & John Minnis

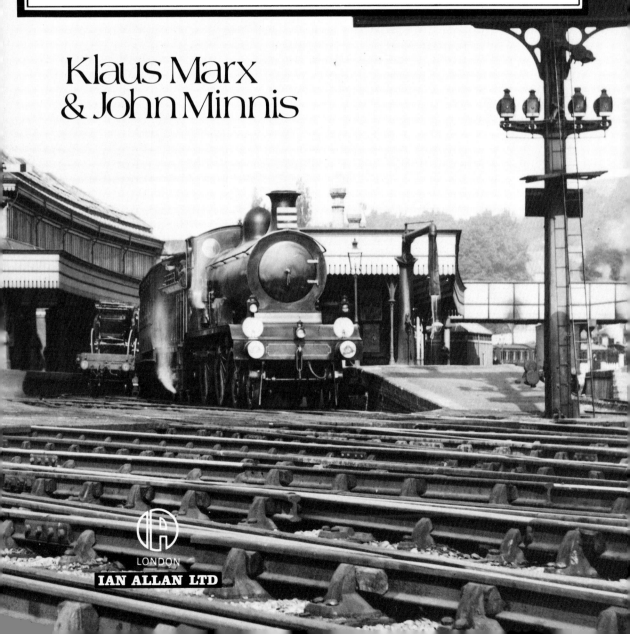

LONDON
IAN ALLAN LTD

First published 1982

ISBN 0 7110 1187 7

Published by Ian Allan Ltd, Shepperton, Surrey;
and printed by Ian Allan Printing Ltd at their works
at Coombelands in Runnymede, England

Below: The elegant lines of a 'B2' compare with the
rather more stocky appearance of a 'B4' in this line up
of engines outside Brighton shed on 4 September 1902.
No 321 *John Rennie* is followed by a 'B4', another 'B2'
and two Singles. *J. R. Minnis Collection*

Contents

Acknowledgements

This album containing much previously unpublished material would not have been possible without the help of a large number of people. For assistance with photographs we are especially indebted to Derek Brough and Maurice Joly for their liberality in making their splendid collections available, and also to R. Halls, C. P. B. Hodgson, Roger Resch, Brian Stephenson, C. W. Underhill and David Wallis together with the Bluebell Archives, Ian Allan Library, Lens of Sutton, the National Railway Museum and the Sussex Archeological Society.

We also have to thank fellow members of the Brighton Circle who have read over parts of the book and made many valuable suggestions; Jonathan Abson, Mike Cruttenden, Arch Overbury and Brian Quemby, and to Derek Brough and Michael Harris for guidance in shaping this book, to Peter Winding for a very explicit map, and to Penny Lowry for grappling with the typing and its sometimes strange terminology.

Finally it is to the memory of those, now sadly no longer with us, who recorded the many delightful photographs reproduced, that this album is dedicated. Credits have been given to the original photographer where known, and apologies are offered should any have been unwittingly omitted. May their careful and painstaking work give much pleasure to those who browse through their masterpieces!

Below: The arrival of the first train at Eastbourne in 1846. The station building depicted in this picture was intended as a temporary structure. It was removed to a different site in Wharf Road and survived until recent times. *From an old print*

Introduction

No other pre-Grouping company, apart from the GWR which retained its identity until nationalisation, has inspired such lasting affection, loyalty and devotion from its many adherents as the London Brighton & South Coast Railway. For the duration of its days the *Southern Railway Magazine*, the continuation of a LSWR precursor, invariably held a historical bias towards all things 'Brighton', and the correspondence columns continued to debate and praise the merits of the old company. There was a similar inbuilt Brighton mechanism in the Stephenson Locomotive Society headed by the great J. N. Maskelyne, where in the pages of its journal, under the editorship of A. G. Williamson, investigation into the Brighton locomotives reached amazing details of research and recording. It was hardly surprising that this eventually led in 1927 to the preservation of Stroudley's 0-4-2 *Gladstone*, the first locomotive to be saved by private enterprise. Again, when the present age of steam railway preservation was born, the first standard gauge passenger scheme to be launched was a section of the Brighton's former Lewes and East Grinstead line by a group of enthusiasts whose pioneer members were predominantly devotees of the Brighton. They set things moving with the acquisition of Stroudley 'Terrier' *Stepney*, and followed this up with the famous *Fenchurch*, R. J. Billinton's 'E4' *Birch Grove* and the 1914 lavish Lancing-built directors' saloon, before the last of the 389 locomotives which had survived into the post-nationalisation period had gone to the scrapheap together with the remaining carriage stock. The latter had been decimated by the prewar electrification of more than half the Company's system, and the last steam locomotives including six of the undying 'Terriers' were withdrawn in 1963. Today the hard core of Brighton enthusiasts reside within the ranks of *The Brighton Circle*, formed in 1974 for the furtherance and publication of original research into the social, technical and economic history of the LB&SCR and its constituents, and whose photography steward, John Minnis, has shared in the production of this present album.

Many authors of previous albums in this field have tried in turn to explain this extraordinary mystique and enduring fascination with the LB&SCR which overlooked many common-day failings at the time and yet made a lasting impression. Was it the homeliness of the names,

and the distinct gamboge livery carried by well over half the locomotives during the 35 years up to 1905, that endeared them to a wide public who still remembered the engines by their names long after they had disappeared? The locomotives somehow had a lifelike quality about their features coupled with the lively pant of a Westinghouse brake pump.

Below: An easy reference pocket card timetable of 1855 printed on behalf of the Epsom and Croydon commuter. Black print on blue card. *K. Marx Collection*

MARCH 1, 1855.

TIMES OF DEPARTURE OF THE CROYDON & LONDON TRAINS.

EPSOM LINE.—Trains marked thus * ARRIVE at CROYDON FROM EPSOM.

DAILY.	UP.	SUNDAY.		DAILY.	DOWN.	SUNDAY.	
7 - 15	C	7 - 15	C	6 - 0	B	6 - 30	D
8 - 0*	C	9 - 15*	C	6 - 45	D	7 - 0	B
8 - 26*	C	10 - 2	B	7 - 0†	C	8 - 15	C
8 - 36	D	10 - 5	D	8 - 15	C	9 - 15†	C
8 - 43	B	10 - 15	C	8 - 20	B	10 - 15	C
9 - 0*	C	1 - 15	C	9 - 15†	C	10 - 30	D
9 - 5	C	1 - 28	D	9 - 30	D	1 - 15†	C
9 - 25*	C	2 - 15*	C	10 - 0	B	1 - 20	B
10 - 0*	C	3 - 15	C	10 - 15	C	2 - 15	C
10 - 15	C	4 - 12	B	11 - 15†	C	3 - 15†	C
10 - 15	C	4 - 15*	C	12 - 0	B	4 - 15	C
10 - 33	C	5 - 15	C	12 - 15	C	5 - 15	C
10 - 49	D	6 - 15	C	1 - 15†	C	5 - 30	D
11 - 15*	C	7 - 15	C	1 - 30	D	6 - 0	B
12 - 15	C	8 - 15*	C	2 - 0	B	6 - 15	C
12 - 30	B	8 - 20	B	2 - 15	C	7 - 15†	C
12 - 43	D	9 - 13	C	3 - 15†	C	8 - 15	C
1 - 15*	C	9 - 15	C	4 - 15	C	9 - 15†	C
2 - 15	C	10 - 15*	C	4 - 45†	C	10 - 15	C
2 - 48	D			5 - 5	B		
3 - 15*	C			5 - 10†	C		
3 - 15	B			5 - 15†	C		
4 - 15	C			5 - 30	D		
4 - 58	B			5 - 45†	C		
5 - 15*	C			6 - 0	B		
5 - 28	D			6 - 15†	C		
6 - 15	C			7 - 15	C		
7 - 15*	C			8 - 15†	C		
8 - 1	B			9 - 15	C		
8 - 15	D			10 - 15†	C		
8 - 43	D			12 - 30	C		
9 - 15*	C						
10 - 15	C						
11 - 45*	C						

TRAINS marked thus † run FROM LONDON TO EPSOM.

All the Croydon Trains have 3rd Class Carriages *except* those with this mark ⁑

RETURN TICKETS are issued to LONDON during the Afternoon of Week Days, from ALL STATIONS on the Croydon & Epsom Line, at REDUCED FARES.

WRIGHT, PRINTER, CROYDON.

The Brighton system was cosy and compact, unlike the straggling routes of some companies. It was triangular in shape with its base firmly planted on the south coast, its apex in London, its perpendicular the Brighton main line, with rough axes of symmetry on either side, Portsmouth complementing Hastings (both of whose coats-of-arms quartered with London and Brighton on the LBSCR crest), Bognor equating with Eastbourne and Littlehampton with Newhaven, the Midhurst line balancing the Cuckoo line in the east, and the Dorking the Oxted line. The lines branching out at Three Bridges provided cross-country links to the 'inner' and 'outer' circle lines that comprised the secondary routes between London and Brighton. The longest main line runs possible by a single train did not exceed 80 miles, and a person living anywhere on the system did not have to travel far to see the majority of engines at work.

Not only was the pattern of the railway map fairly uniform, but so too was the landscape. By Croydon most of the metropolitan suburbia had been left behind, and the trains worked on rising grades into the foothills of the ridge of the North Downs, the three major routes tunnelling under them at Mickleham, Merstham and Oxted, then through the greensand ridge of the Weald embracing the former extensive St Leonards Forest, piercing it at Balcombe, Sharpthorne, Crowborough and Rotherfield, and yet again through the splendid South Downs, burrowing at Amberley, Clayton and Lewes. Within the triangular area the company held a virtual monopoly and, apart from the Tunbridge Wells-Hastings and Midhurst-Petersfield lines, was *the* railway of Sussex.

The LBSCR rated as the ninth of the 'Big Nine' with 457 route miles including 100 of single track, and was basically a passenger line which ran an intense service Londonwards. From early days both suburban and main line commuter traffic was encouraged, together with all the economics of season tickets which averaged £643 for each route mile in 1910, and indicated the degree of residential development taking place. The country lines served areas of large estates and a high class clientele, and E. L. Ahrons, the noted locomotive historian, was perhaps justified in writing: 'The management naturally considered their railway to be a first class line and they backed up their opinion by making the best trains first class only at super first class fares!' The directors' opinion was not shared by the unfortunate second and third class passengers. The Company was served by some astute chairmen commencing with Rowland Hill, who was one of the first to introduce excursion trains. The now almost legendary excursion train on Easter Monday, 1844, made London Bridge to Brighton in $4\frac{1}{2}$ hours, starting with four engines and 45 coaches

and arrived with six engines and 57 coaches. Samuel Laing who, restoring solvency after the financial collapse of the mid-1860s, held sway in the mid-Victorian period, besides pulling off some tactical coups infilling the East Sussex area to counter South Eastern Railway threats, was largely instrumental in the removal of the Crystal Palace to Sydenham. The introduction of one of the pioneer suburban overhead electrification schemes saw traffic double in the first three months, and in 1912 the Crystal Palace group of lines recorded a 70% increase and kept the threat of the tram at bay most effectively prior to World War 1. The electrification programme laid the foundations for the later development of an intensive network of medium and long distance commuter traffic. Imposed upon this was the special boat train and forces traffic centring on Newhaven and Portsmouth, the former becoming the base of a fleet of efficient railway steamers running cross-Channel services.

The goods traffic was in a minor key, but nevertheless prospered in bringing the products of the industrial north, especially coal, to the southern Home Counties, and served the metropolis with the produce of the land, in particular milk and fruit and timber. The war period saw an intense use of Newhaven as a munitions port, and permission for a further batch of 'K' class 2-6-0s had to be sought.

Most will remember the Brighton for its locomotives and the influence their designers had on the history of the railway. The first of real stature was John Chester Craven, an old time autocrat, dour and taciturn, who is credited with the building of Brighton Works. As O. J. Morris put it: 'His creative genius ran riot in designing engines', which were built on a one-off basis with specific duties in mind, and even a series was not identical. The golden age was undoubtedly that of the period of William Stroudley, officious yet kindly, and venerated by his men whose dignity he enhanced by allocating each man a machine and blazoning the owner's name in the cab for all to read. W. G. Tilling who produced a forerunner of the later Ian Allan ABCs, talks of his 'genius', and according to F. C. Hambleton 'The finest designer of the lot. For beauty with commonsense he had no equal, and his detail work was simply super'. Stroudley was a strange mixture of the conservative and the innovator; bogies, injectors or machine-riveted boilers were out, but he was the first in Britain to cast two cylinders in one piece. His modernisation of Brighton Works produced adequate plant for the next 30 years. The standard of workmanship was undisputed and filtered through to the system as a whole which enjoyed one of its better periods of timekeeping. In the opinion of Ralph Stent, a Brighton antiquarian, 'Locomotives, rolling stock

and staff combined to make it a ''3C'' concern — Clean — Courteous — Certain! — making one *want to travel'*.

The yellow livery was perpetuated by Robert Billinton, but with bogies and injectors introduced, and it was his 'B4' class locomotive *Holyrood* that ran Victoria-Brighton in 48min 40sec in 1903. Trained by Stroudley as his chief draughtsman (1870-78), he is perhaps given less credit as a designer than he deserves. Whereas he had brought with him the influence of the Midland Railway, his successor, Douglas Earle Marsh, introduced that of the Great Northern. He made some sweeping changes in livery, introduced superheating, locomotive exchanges with the LNWR in 1909, and among his better designs his Atlantics and 'I3' class

express tank engines. Lawson Billinton, R. J. Billinton's son, developed the Marsh 'J' class tanks into Baltics with 22in×28in cylinders, the largest in the country, and introduced the 'K' class Moguls, the most powerful locomotives on the line. Some traditions persisted to the end, the Billinton cab, Stroudley's tyre profile and the Westinghouse brake valve. With such an attractive variety it was small wonder that F. Burtt, a former LBSCR draughtsman and author, could write on the eve of nationalisation: 'Interest in the locomotives of the former LBSCR seems to be daily more widespread'.

Turning to the coaching stock, examples of the early period were somewhat spartan and lightweight, but it took some years for the public to adapt to the luxurious Pullman cars, first introduced in 1875. The typical Brighton arc roof survived into the Marsh era. The latter's 'Balloon' coaches were the first with elliptical roofs, soon followed by main line stock, and later by the newly designed electric stock. Following the Newark brake trials the Westinghouse brake was adopted on the system. Slip coaches were another

Brighton first, commencing in 1858; electric lighting another with the Pullman cars of 1881 lit from accumulators only, the suburban coach sets of 1883 by dynamo and battery, and the 1898 'Pullman Limited' from miniature 'Pullman Pups'.

But it was in signalling that the Brighton pioneered the way with the first semaphore anywhere at New Cross in 1842, the first interlocked semaphores the following year at Bricklayers Arms Junction, and interlocked with points at Norwood Junction in 1844; the first notched distants anywhere appeared at the latter place in 1872. Messrs Saxby and Farmer were both Brighton employees, and developed a monopoly from 1863 till 1904. Block working was complete by 1874 and interlocking by 1877. Platform distants were introduced at London Bridge in 1878 with mechanical route indicators, and Brighton was enlarged and resignalled in the same way in 1883 with its huge South Box of 240 levers in one frame. Sykes 'Lock and Block' came in the 1880s and Coligny Welch signals in 1906, and improvements and adaptations continued in the new century. The Brighton signalboxes repay study, developing from the original type with slotted post signals into a variety of styles. The most common type had neat toplights over the windows while others had bargeboards and finials adorning them. From the turn of the century boxes had gabled ends rather than the hipped roofs of earlier days.

Notable architectural and structural features on the system include the classical lines on which David Mocatta raised the original main line with the viaducts at the Ouse valley and the equally impressive one laid out on a curve at London Road, and of course Clayton Tunnel, the gothic gateway to the south coast, originally whitewashed and reportedly lit from Hassocks gasworks. Unusual features were its moveable bridges at Ford, Southerham and Deptford, and its covered ways at Cane Hill and Pimlico. The stations were in general superior to those on neighbouring lines, from the early classical stucco of the 1840s to the red brick type that followed. Again the 1860s saw simple yet adequate buildings, followed by more ornate ones in the 1880s, some becoming quite extravagant and boasting stained glass windows. In the late 1890s came the 'super suburban style' with lavish waiting rooms, culminating in the crowning glory of the new style Victoria with its double length platforms.

The many achievements and attractiveness of the LBSCR gave it such an aura that there was, and indeed still is, a human tendency to overlook its many foibles and shortcomings. Perhaps most notable among these was the unpunctuality and late running chiefly due to congested junctions and, until 1900, a shared main line north of

Redhill, also generally undistinguished speeds if compared with the route timings of other major companies, and poor third class travel during the early years.

Moreover, in spite of being a pioneer in electrification, electric lighting, signalling and continuous brakes, the LBSCR paid the price by backing the wrong horse on each case, and it suffered accordingly. While the Brighton adopted the Stroudley Rusbridge lighting system, the majority of other railways fixed on Stone's system. While it went to great trouble in selecting overhead AC as the best system for electrification (and which hindsight has proved correct), later schemes went for the DC third rail. It selected the Westinghouse air brake when the vacuum brake was coming into popular use, and it chose slotted post signals and rotating 'Dolly lights' when spectacle arm posts were becoming the norm.

The visible relics of the Brighton have shrunk in the post-World War 2 period, but much of the network still remains open despite minor casualties in the rural areas. While most of the engineering structures survive, the rationalisation and modernisation of stations has thinned out those most visible to the lingering passenger. Dorking is a most recent example. However, a restoration back to Brighton originals is taking place on the Bluebell Railway with its two stations and compatible signals, its three ex-LBSCR locomotives, directors' saloon, fruit van and open wagon. *Gladstone* and 'Terrier' *Boxhill* can be viewed in the National Railway Museum at York, while other 'Terriers' survive on preserved lines at Rolvenden, Minehead, Bressingham and especially on the Isle of Wight where the centre at Haven Street has three operational Brighton coaches.

Perhaps the largest and most lasting tribute to the LBSCR is the Sussex of today in which, according to John Lowerson in a recent book, 'The LBSCR represented the peak of Victorian industrial achievement: there was no other single concern which could rival it'. The area today, with the full grown Brighton even sporting a First Division football team, the ports of Newhaven, Shoreham and Littlehampton, the retiring resorts of Eastbourne, Worthing and Bognor, the dormitory and new towns of mid-Sussex, close to the main line, the suburban consolidation of South London, all were largely the product of a railway that still lives in the memories of those who worked or travelled on it. The ranks of those who can recall the famous Stroudley 'gamboge' livery are indeed few today, and yet the fascination remains amongst those of later generations who can only recapture the atmosphere and hold of the Brighton in an album of this nature.

Klaus Marx

The Brighton's Photographic Heritage

On the whole the LBSCR was well served by its photographers. The supply of official photographs is a little disappointing and the LBSCR lacks the matchless collections of negatives of the Great Western, the LNWR or the NER. On the other hand, there exists a wide variety of pictures from non-official sources, both amateur and commercial. O. J. Morris once stated that he had seen a photograph of every Stroudley LBSCR locomotive with its name on except nine, and the coverage of stations too is remarkably complete.

A point worth making, and one that applies to railways generally, is that one needs to consider why a particular photograph was taken. Railway enthusiasts, or 'railwayacs' as the *Railway Magazine* of the day quaintly termed them, were as a rule only interested in photographing locomotives and trains. They would occasionally take a picture of an item of rolling stock if it was exceptional in some way, for example an elderly service vehicle or one involved in an accident, though most carriage and wagon pictures were taken for official purposes. A number of station photographs are official but the great majority were taken by local and national photographic firms as part of a series of postcards depicting items of interest in the locality. The stations of which few photographs exist are generally those which do not have a village in the immediate vicinity and those in the poorer inner London districts where the market for sales was perhaps smaller.

The cumbersome nature of the available equipment meant that amateur work was not widespread until the 1890s. There is a pleasant description of one Sussex photographer of the period travelling around with his assistant in a pony and trap to take his pictures.

The earliest known photographs to have survived are a number taken at Brighton in 1858-9. Several are reproduced in this book. Quite a few Craven locomotives were photographed in the 1860s, a number of fine views being in the Morris collection and that of the Locomotive Publishing Company. Unfortunately, they fall into the category of 'anonymous masterpieces' for little is known of their origins. A few of the LPC views may well be the work of R. E. Bleasdale, the first prolific locomotive photographer whose name has come down. Most of the early locomotive views tend to be located at the major sheds of Battersea, New Cross or Brighton, due to the

previously mentioned problem of transporting bulky plate cameras.

A figure well known outside the purely railway sphere and locally enjoying a high reputation was Edward Reeves of Lewes who took a number of very early pictures at Lewes station. Some of these photographs are held by the Sussex Archeological Society at Lewes and copies of others appear in several collections.

Another Lewes man, E. J. Bedford FRPS, produced what can be considered from both the artistic and technical points of view, the finest photographs of the LBSCR. Bedford was a schoolmaster at Brighton School of Art, one of whose governors was William Stroudley, and it is almost certain that he used this connection to gain access to the railway around Lewes. His interest in photography extended far beyond railways and he was well known locally as secretary to the photographic society, as a member of the board of the natural history society and as curator of the town's museum. His views of moving trains in the Lewes area in the 1880s are technically remarkable as some of the earliest really sharp pictures portraying the railway in action, and a general generous selection are included in this album. Bedford was active over a long period from c1880 to the first electric trains through Lewes in 1935. John E. Kite in *Vintage Album* recounts that he was so jealous of his pictures that he had to be present when prints were taken off his negatives in case a second copy was taken without his knowledge.

Another early photographer of moving trains was Dr T. F. Budden who seems to have been the most active on the Brighton system around the turn of the century when he took many pictures in the vicinity of Balham Intermediate signalbox. G. F. Burtt, the company's unofficial locomotive historian, was taking photographs from the 1890s onwards. Employed by the LBSCR as a draughtsman, he also acted as official photographer to some extent in the years 1906-14, posing many locomotives on the Crumbles siding and near the Eastbourne locomotive shed. He also issued his own prints as postcards marked 'Photographed and printed by G. F. Burtt, Ringmer, Nr Lewes, Sussex'.

An almost legendary name to Brighton devotees, J. N. Maskelyne, took many photographs in the Edwardian era. W. G. Tilling, the third member with the last mentioned of what one might almost term the 'Brighton Trinity', has

his name on a good many old prints, but whether he actually took the photographs or simply published the work of others is not clear. He may in fact have taken many of the Brighton company's official portraits. His cards of excellent quality are hard to find today, a point he has in common with another great character, the fabulous E. Pouteau who sold copy prints in the way that Real Photographs do today. Stories about his seedy little shop in the Grays Inn Road can be found in Kite's book and elsewhere.

Dr A. C. Hovenden, a friend of Maskelyne who lived for many years in North Sheen, collaborated with another doctor whose name is better known today, John Bradbury Winter, in creating some fine Brighton models. He took many photographs from the 1890s onward which, while not of the highest quality, are of the more unusual subject.

Many of the pictures in this album are the work of the Bennett brothers who, based at Brighton, went off on bicycles, often along with another photographer, Ralph Stent, on weekend photographic excursions. Their quality was high and they also tended to compose attractive pictures showing the train in the landscape as opposed to the usual three-quarter frontal view. The brothers V. and T. Chambers roamed more widely and distinguished their work by frustratingly writing on each negative the date, their initials and the negative number. Other photographers of the pre-1914 period were H. Glazebrook, 'T. Lens' (whose real name was Parker), the original Lens of Sutton, R. W. T.

Collins active in the coastal area and E. T. Vyse responsible for many action pictures on the main line in the Coulsdon area. E. S. Hallett was a photographer who, like the Bennetts, secured attractive photographs of trains in the landscape.

Professional photographers covered the whole system recording the great majority of its stations on postcards. W. H. Smith & Son included many Brighton stations on their Kingsway Real Photo series, recognisable by the title in the border below the subject and a number prefaced by the latter 'S'. A. H. Homewood of Burgess Hill issued many cards, some coloured, and some real photographs, while F. W. Spry of Littlehampton took many pictures in that area that later ended up in the Morris collection.

The best known of train photographers also paid their visits to the LBSCR. Both F. E. Mackay and H. Gordon Tidey took some excellent pictures, albeit in a very limited range of locations. Mackay took most of his pictures at the Balham Intermediate site while Tidey chose various locations, among the most favoured being Purley, Dorking, Hassocks and Patcham. C. Laundy was also active on the main line near Purley from around 1913 to beyond 1923.

The end of World War 1 saw the emergence of another celebrated Brighton figure, O. J. Morris of Beulah Hill, known as 'the man in black' or 'the professor'. Morris was a fine photographer who would take almost any subject including the off-beat items that others neglected, although he may equally be remembered for the way in which he collected together many old negatives and copied old prints to produce a collection of singular interest. He issued these commercially as 'Super Sepia' postcards, the praises of which he sang in neat lists printed by himself on an Adana. His comments were justifiable however as the results were superb. 'O. J.' was involved with Ian Allan Ltd in their early days as the first editor of *Trains Illustrated,* and he kept up a steady Brighton flavour in the *Southern Railway Magazine.* On his death in 1962 the negatives passed to Lens of Sutton.

Many of the Brighton aficionados were founder members of the Stephenson Locomotive Society who arranged visits to LBSCR sheds. One such individual was L. E. Brailsford who took a wide selection of views. He had, however, one annoying habit; he used to write all over his photographs and unfortunately his handwriting was not of the most stylish variety. B. Whicher took some unusual views on the main line in the company's last years, and these are also held by Lens of Sutton. H. M. Madgwick, from whose collection a number of the pictures in this album have been taken, commenced photography just before the Grouping.

This account makes no claim to be exhaustive,

Above: A 3rd class pass of 1881 — coloured pink in the original. *K. Marx Collection*

but it is hoped it will shed some light on a neglected topic and provide a little information about the men to whose skill such a debt is owed today. The whereabouts of the negatives of many of the photographers mentioned are unknown. Some have no doubt shared the fate of Pouteau's, sold for use as vegetable garden cloches or perhaps just thrown away. Many prints however have been copied over the years and there is much satisfaction to be derived from the detective work involved in trying to determine the original photographer whose name is all too often consigned to oblivion.

John Minnis

The Craven Era

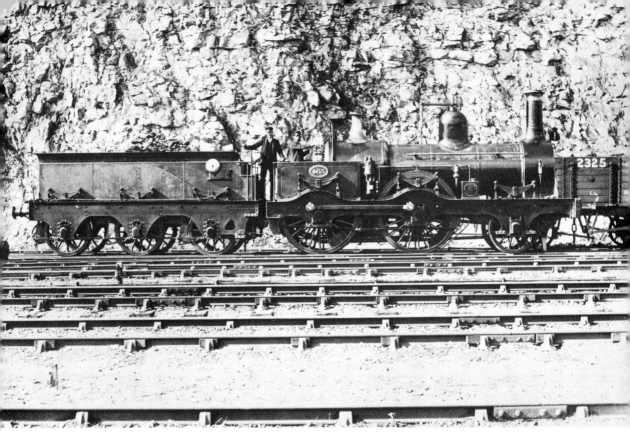

Above left: John Chester Craven, his wife and daughter pose in front of newly built 'West End' 2-4-0 well tank No 15 at Brighton in May 1858, the first positively dated LBSCR photograph to come to light.
O. J. Morris Collection/Ian Allan Library (IAL)

Left: One of the most successful of Craven's designs were the 12 handsome Beyer Peacock 2-4-0s of 1864. Stroudley made few alterations to them other than painting them in his usual ochre livery. No 188 poses with crew and shed foreman in this magnificent portrait taken at Battersea shed in the 1870s. The tender displays the Stroudley/Rusbridge warning device. *J. R. Minnis Collection*

Above: No 465 formerly 185 of the same series photographed at Brighton between September 1889 when it was renumbered and October 1890 when it was withdrawn. *IAL*

Right: A most unusual rear view of another Craven 2-4-0 on an up train at Uckfield c1890. The 1882 signalbox is still there to this day while the picture forms a delightful Victorian period piece.
J. R. Minnis Collection

Above: A down Brighton train bursting out of Merstham tunnel. While of indifferent quality, this is the only known photograph of one of Craven's locomotives in motion and at some speed. *D. J. W. Brough Collection*

Below: The turntable at the old Eastbourne roundhouse was a favourite spot for locomotive photographs. No 476 *Arundel*, a handsome Nasmyth Wilson single of 1867, poses with crew and running shed foreman between 1881 and 1889 when the engine was withdrawn. The flower bed with its whitened stone border is typical of the little embellishments that staff of this period would make.
Rixon Bucknall Collection/IAL

Below: For freight working, Craven designed several series of 0-6-0s. One of the earlier Brighton built examples, No 394 (old 211) of 1865 stands at New Cross shed in the 1880s. The elaborate frontage of Aspinall's Enamel Works and the boarding of the platform fence of New Cross station are to be seen in the background of a vast number of LBSC pictures. *Locomotive Publishing Company (LPC)/IAL*

Bottom: Craven six-coupled goods, built as No 224 in June 1866, underwent several renumberings, a feature of the Brighton at this period, frustrating to later historians but useful in narrowing down the dating of locomotive photographs. By March 1895 it had become another number, 465, and this fine shot at Ford Junction must have been taken in the next six months before its scrapping in October 1895. The first vehicle is a Stroudley brake van, one of a number built with lantern roofs. *Locomotive and General Photographs (LGRP) (By kind permission of David & Charles)*

Top: New England Road bridges, Brighton in 1858. The central bridge with its separate arches over the pavements, is the original London and Brighton Railway structure, while the iron structure further down the hill carries the line to Brighton's low level goods yard. On the embankment to the left of the bridges is the original Montpelier Junction signalbox, comprising a hut mounted on a raised platform, a direct descendant of Gregory's pioneer of 1842. The works and their access road which goes across the tracks are seen on the right. *O. J. Morris Collection/IAL*

Above: The western approaches to Brighton in 1859 as seen from the tunnel over the Worthing line. The extent of the works and running sheds which extend the length of the picture are clear. Filling the centre is the remains of the old chalk hill which was removed over a number of years. The site was later chosen by Stroudley to build the new Brighton locomotive sheds. *O. J. Morris Collection/Lens of Sutton*

Above: This and the following three pictures form a panoramic view of Brighton station and its approaches. They were taken from a house in Terminus Road in the spring or autumn of 1871. The foreground building was used as the paintshop for many years and is still extant today. Montpelier Junction box was rebuilt by John Saxby in 1862 and is of the characteristic pattern of the day, raised as if on stilts and with signal posts passing through the box. The Lewes line curves away on Mocatta's beautiful London Road viaduct. A ticket collector's platform runs alongside the works. There were many complaints at the time about the delays caused to passengers by this practice at Brighton.
Lens of Sutton

Below: The works and the old running sheds shortly before their removal to the other side of the tracks. An assortment of Craven stock fills the foreground. Some of it dates from the 1850s while there is some later stock with tumblehome to the sides. The most recent vehicle is a three compartment brake 3rd of c1866 in the back row. The lantern roofs of the passenger brake vans are much in evidence. The old locomotive shed is in the centre with the erecting shop beyond the Brighton North box. Amidst the green fields by the viaduct is the site of the future Brighton London Road station.
Lens of Sutton

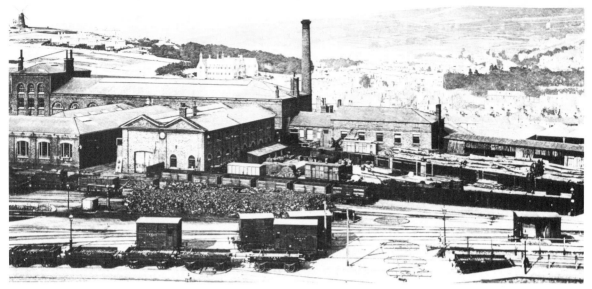

Above: The approach to the main line platforms with a fine variety of rolling stock. In the foreground stand six open carriage trucks, from left to right, Nos 47 built 1864, 74, 20 of 1849, 43 and 40 built by Smith and Dagley in 1846 for £97 10s each. Behind are five horseboxes, including from the left No 117 built 1869, an unidentified vehicle without grooms' accommodation and not dissimilar to early Great Western vehicles, and 37 of 1856; then, a line of coal wagons belonging to Booth Brothers of Eastwood, Notts and two rather quaint coke wagons with lattice work sides of c1851. In the yard stand two very early vehicles. The nearer appears to be a 3rd converted to departmental use and the other a grounded body which may be a Parliamentary coach. The presence of large tree trunks in the saw mill yard emphasise the almost universal use of wood in rolling stock construction in 1871. The three-storey structure on the left side of the works is the office of the redoubtable Mr Craven. The line of wagon turntables across the platform ends is a characteristic feature of the railway scene enabling the horseboxes and carriage trucks to be transferred from platform to platform. *Lens of Sutton*

Below: The old low overall station roofs swept away in the great rebuilding of 1882/3, are prominent in this view. A couple of one horse delivery vans are parked in the carriage road. Behind stands a road van bearing the legend LBSC TOOL BOX in the outside framing, which indicates that it and the three plank wagon next to it form part of the breakdown train. In the yard stands an early version of the familiar round ended merchandise wagon, inscribed LB & SCR 432, the earliest evidence of the company's lettering style for wagons.
Lens of Sutton

Below: The site of the 1846 terminus at Friars Walk, Lewes, photographed about 1860. The goods shed, which was then newly constructed still stands to this day.
From the Reeves Collection — reproduced by courtesy of the Sunday Times *and the Sussex Archaeological Society*

Bottom: The London platforms of the 1857 Lewes station captured about 1860. A beautifully posed picture with the elderly gentleman on the left apparently reading to the small boy beside him. Note the rather primitive platform accommodation and the massive cast iron water crane. Two horseboxes and a carriage truck stand in the yard.
From the Reeves Collection — reproduced by courtesy of the Sunday Times *and the Sussex Archaeological Society*

Above: Lewes c1860 probably photographed by Edward Reeves. The second station of 1857 was built in an unusual and most attractive Swiss Chalet style. Vehicles evident in the small yard in the angle formed by the junction of the Brighton and London lines are again horseboxes and carriage trucks. A Single stands on the coast line platform. The short, low platforms and the absence of signals are noteworthy. The platform canopy spanning the bay was similar to that at Barnham Junction. *Lens of Sutton*

Below: The south end of Clayton tunnel c1860 showing the primitive signalling used. The red flag was displayed by the signalman when the line was not clear. A distant signal preceded the tunnel mouth by 350 yards. The disastrous accident of 25 August 1861 in which 23 people lost their lives occurred soon after the photograph was taken.
H. M. Madgwick Collection/IAL

Above: 2-2-2 well tank *Merton* stands in the Brighton platform at Wimbledon some time between 1871 when first named and 1877 when laid aside. Built in May 1852 No 14 was the first locomotive built at Brighton Works and was renumbered 278 in June 1874. The first vehicle with its lantern roof is a c1860 brake 3rd followed by two 3rds of similar date. The platform lamp is a fine example of cast iron work.
H. M. Madgwick Collection/IAL

Centre left: A Craven designed cattle wagon 1786 at Lovers Walk sidings in 1882. The vehicle is depicted very much in operating condition; the company was very liberal with its use of limewash to the point where the livery was almost obscured. The primitive brake gear with one wooden brake block acting on one wheel is typical of the period as are the massive wooden heads to the buffers and the safety chains.
LBSCR official/J. R. Minnis Collection

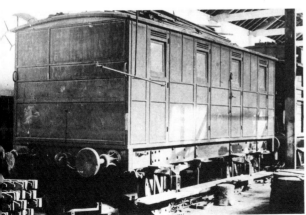

Bottom left: Typifying the rather miserable accommodation provided for third class passengers is this four wheel third of c1852 photographed in 1910 in service use at Brighton Works. The unfortunate passengers had no windows to look out of save the droplights in each door. The vehicle has been little altered and shows well the stylistic features of the period, flat sides with rectangular beading and very shallow arc roof. *H. M. Madgwick Collection/IAL*

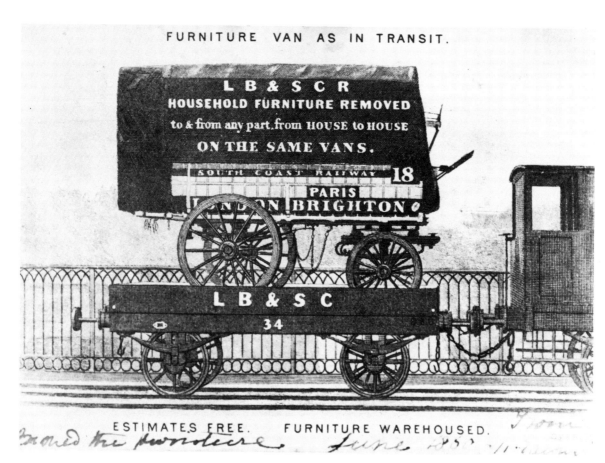

L B & S C R
HOUSEHOLD FURNITURE REMOVED
to & from any part. from HOUSE to HOUSE
ON THE SAME VANS.
SOUTH COAST RAILWAY 18
PARIS
LONDON BRIGHTON

L B & S C
34

ESTIMATES FREE.   FURNITURE WAREHOUSED.

Above: The problem of transferring goods from road
vehicles to rail and vice versa is one that has received
much attention in recent years. This line drawing
reproduced from advertising material believed to date
from 1860 shows an early attempt to solve the problem.
The open carriage truck, which is of early date bears a
horse dray used for removals work. The service could
be seen as a distant forerunner of the American
'piggyback' mode of operation.
National Railway Museum (NRM), Crown Copyright

Right: In common with other railways, the LBSCR once
it passed the stage of signals mounted on a platform
with a hut shown earlier, erected structures raised up
on massive baulks of timber with twin signal posts
passing right through the box. The Lewes box shown
here in the 1870s still in its original form was one of the
earliest to be built. The two men on the maintenance
platform give a good idea of the height of the
structure.   *E. J. Bedford/M. Joly Collection*

Left: Folly Hill, on the main line between Haywards Heath and Wivelsfield was built in 1863 and was a late survivor of the 'stilts' boxes, not being replaced until 1908. It is in final condition with the signal posts cut off at the box roof. *M. Joly Collection*

Below: The end of the Craven era is heralded by this line of goods locomotives at Horley awaiting scrap, probably in 1896. The leading engine No 468 is the only 'live' one and is one of the final batch of the type built by Slaughter. The others are Brighton built, the third being No 463 and have their numbers and weights painted roughly on them, the standard procedure before locomotives were sold for scrap. The appearance of the engines is not very prepossessing with their stove pipe chimneys and crude side plates to the weather boards. In the background are the stucco Tudor style down side buildings of Mocatta's original London and Brighton station. *Lens of Sutton*

The Stroudley Age

Above: A cartoon of Stroudley, from a periodical called *The Brightonian*. The original is titled *Locomotive Department LB & SCR*, but the emphasis would appear to be on signalling, judging by the slotted post example behind his right arm while his left hand holds a document entitled 'Patent Railway Signals'. The Brighton Company had a good reputation for signalling. *M. Joly Collection*

Left: William Stroudley, beside 'Terrier' No 40 *Brighton* on its return from the Paris Exhibition in 1878. His reputation as a dapper figure is much in evidence. Tightly furled umbrella, silk hat and gloves, the epitome of a man at the height of his profession. *Lens of Sutton*

Above right: The first August Bank Holiday 1871. Engines assemble at Lovers Walk in the evening ready to take the excursionists back to London. The figure in the top hat standing by the locomotive on the right is said to be William Stroudley. The line up includes on the left No 203 the new *Sussex*, No 255 *Hastings* and next to it 2-4-0 No 248 *Hove*. The line of wagons is standing on the sharp incline to the lower goods depot. The very early disc signal is noteworthy. Those familiar with the London Road area beneath the viaduct carrying the East Coast line today will find the bare grass fields striking indeed. *O. J. Morris Collection/Lens of Sutton*

Right: East Grinstead has had three stations on as many sites. This is the second of 1866, with the station buildings adjacent to the road bridge and platforms slightly to the north of what later became known as the upper goods yard. The stationmaster in full regalia formally hands the token for the Three Bridges section to the crew of a Craven 2-4-0 while passengers pose, though some were unable to keep quite still. The buildings which were demolished after the opening of the third station in 1883 closely resembled those at Holmwood. *J. R. Minnis Collection*

27

Above: Brighton c1880. While the station still retains the low pitched roofs, the layout altogether looks much more modern than in the 1872 views. Gone are the wagon turntables and the platforms have been considerably lengthened. The clock tower is a prominent feature that disappeared in the rebuilding. Stroudley's clerestory mail van set stands on one road while a 'C' class 0-6-0 is on the right. On the left is a late Craven 2-4-0. *Lens of Sutton*

Below: Eastbourne in the 1880s looking towards the station. The signalbox and the rear of the roundhouse are evident in the background. One of Stroudley's 2-4-0s is in steam while together with some Stroudley carriages, there is a brake 3rd and a five compartment 3rd of 1866 vintage. The line branching off past the houses of Ashford Square is the siding leading to the Duke of Devonshire's Yard. *Lens of Sutton*

Top: Chichester looking west from South Street Crossing in the early 1880s, still with its overall roof which was replaced in 1894. The handsome classical station building on the right dates from the opening of the line and was demolished when the station was rebuilt in 1958. The East signalbox, seen here in the foreground, also enjoyed longevity; erected in 1875, it was closed in 1973. *From the late E. Wallis' Collection*

Above: Horley looking towards London in 1886. The station depicted here was situated to the north of the present site, the change being made on the line widening of 1905. New works including the up station building and the canopy on the down side had just been completed. A typical slotted post Saxby & Farmer signal forms the down starter. *LBSCR Official/IAL*

Above: Saxby & Farmer's 280 lever installation, in two lever frames 'back to back', at London Bridge North Cabin was brought into use in 1879 and was later altered to tappet locking, remaining at work until 1928. This had the 1874 'grid iron' interlocking so long used on the railway, and superseded smaller boxes erected in 1866.
C. P. B. Hodgson Collection/Westinghouse Brake & Signal Co

Below: The exterior of the 1878 North Cabin at London Bridge terminus and showing platform home and starting signals and route indicators, believed to have been used here for the first time. The distant arms were provided to indicate whether there was another train already at the far end of the platform, being lowered only when the line was clear to the buffers. The lamps are of the original Saxby pattern, but about 1897 carrying spectacles were adopted with a white stripe painted on the red face instead of a black one.
C. P. B Hodgson Collection/Westinghouse Brake & Signal Co

Above: One of the smallest signalboxes on the system, Haydens Lane on the LBSCR/LSWR joint line to Wimbledon. The station nameboard is of the LSWR pattern but the box plate is of the LBSCR enamelled type. The station was renamed Haydens Road in 1889 so the picture presumably predates that year.
H. M. Madgwick Collection/IAL

Centre left: Nearing completion in 1888 is Lewes Junction signalbox, a large example of the 1876 design, distinguished by the attractive string course of darker brickwork.
From the Reeves Collection — reproduced by courtesy of the Sunday Times *and the Sussex Archaeological Society*

Bottom left: No 207 *Freshwater* of 1876 at Tunbridge Wells shed not long after the shed was constructed in 1890. The tall lamps mounted on a post similar to that used for signals was a standard design. The livery of the shed doors, a two tone buff, is characteristic. *Lens of Sutton*

Top: Lingfield prior to opening in May 1884, one of a series of photographs taken for the contractor building the line. The scene has the bare look that distinguished new lines for years after their construction. The opening of Lingfield Racecourse led to major alterations to the still new station in 1894 when the down platform was converted to an island. The signalbox is of the most numerous type with round cornered toplights introduced in 1876. *Lens of Sutton*

Above: Cooks Pond viaduct further down the line to East Grinstead. Again the structure is brand new, making one realise that the railway produced scars on the landscape similar to a modern motorway.
H. M. Madgwick Collection/Bluebell Archives

Above: The down 'Pullman Limited' headed by a
Stroudley 0-4-2 powers through Preston Park at the
turn of the century. The train consisted of the two
Pullman Pups, and the cars *Victoria, Beatrice, Princess
of Wales, Duchess of York* and *Her Majesty*. Note the
particularly fine examples of the old slotted post signals.
One of the arms of the signal on the right has vanished
into its slot. *LPC/IAL*

Below: 2-4-0 No 602 *Goodwood* on a train of Stroudley
four- and six-wheel carriages. The locomotive was
eking out the last few years of its existence, working
from Brighton when photographed in 1901. The last
survivor of the 'Belgravia' class it was withdrawn the
following year. *M. P. Bennett/Bluebell Archives*

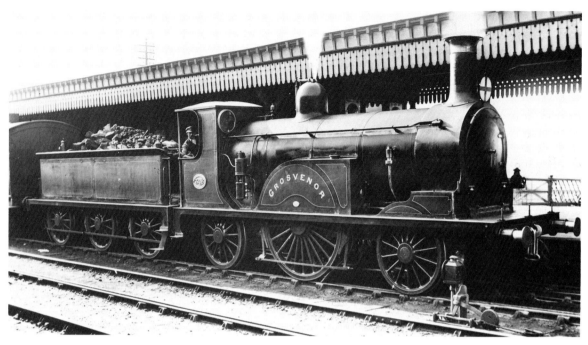

Above: No 326 *Grosvenor*, Stroudley's first 2-2-2, much larger than the 'G' class that followed it and the only one of its type. The elaborate platform roof valancing identifies the location as Portsmouth Harbour in 1903. *O. J. Morris Collection/Lens of Sutton*

Below: *Martello* as renumbered with transfers in 1901, pauses from shunting at New Cross in the early 1900s. A collection of lamps grace the footplate at the front while the driver's lunch bag rests on the tanks. The 'Terrier' in its rebuilt form survives at Bressingham Steam Museum today. *Lens of Sutton*

Top: The largest class of locomotives numerically south of the Thames were Stroudley's 'D' class, comprising 125 engines designed to handle suburban and branch line traffic. No 277 *Slinfold* of 1879 is seen from the footpath that runs along the line near South Croydon. The usual repository for firing shovels and pricking rods on tank locomotives was on top of the side tank next to the boiler, safely steadied by the tank filler cap. *LPC/IAL*

Above: Stroudley designed a tender version of the 'D1' for mixed traffic use. Although capable engines which in their heyday hauled the main line expresses including regular turns on the 'Grand Vitesse' workings, their lives were far shorter than most of the corresponding tanks. No 300 *Lyons* poses in the locomotive shed yard at New Cross in 1882. *O. J. Morris Collection/Bluebell Archives*

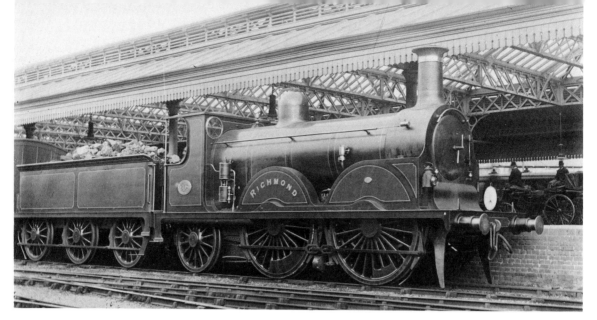

Top: An enlarged version of the design formed the antecedent of the celebrated 'Gladstones'. No 608 *Richmond* at Eastbourne between 1900 and 1903. Eastbourne was rebuilt on a grand scale in 1886 as is clear from the roof spanning the cab road.
M. P. Bennett/Bluebell Archives

Above: No 210 *Cornwall* of the same class, built 1879, captured with exquisite precision on the turntable of the 1857 Lewes station in the 1880s. Behind the front buffers is a good example of one of the Brighton's third class carriages of the 1850s. *Edward Reeves*

Top right: 'G' class Single on the down Newhaven boat train crossing the River Ouse near Southerham Junction c1891. The train includes Stroudley full brakes, the two six-wheel lavatory composites, Nos 271/2 built to diagram 42/84 in 1882 and American Pullman *Victoria* in original condition with open verandahs. Until the turn of the century toilet facilities were virtually unknown on regular LBSCR services.
E. J. Bedford/M. J. Cruttenden Collection

Centre right: Another view of the Newhaven boat train with 'B1' No 174 *Fratton* south of Southerham Junction. The train represents the epitome of the Stroudley era, being composed entirely of Stroudley carriages; its third vehicle is one of the lavatory composites seen in the previous photograph. Note that someone has left an oil lamp cover open.
E. J. Bedford/M. J. Cruttenden Collection

Bottom right: A royal race special near Lewes, carrying Edward, Prince of Wales, displaying the royal 'feathers' and headcode, and hauled by *Grosvenor* on 20 June 1891. The stock comprises Diagram 47 brakes at each end, with two six-wheel firsts next to them. The third vehicle is the 1877 Stroudley Royal saloon and next to that is a 1st Class saloon.
E. J. Bedford/M. J. Cruttenden Collection

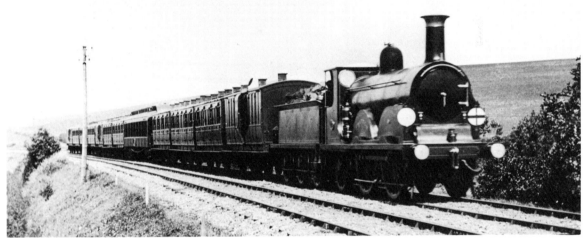

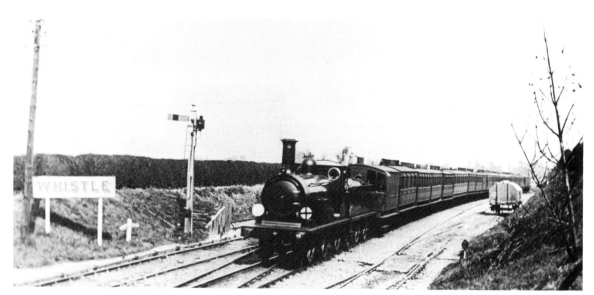

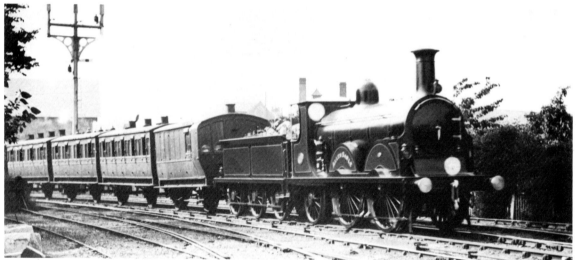

Top left: A 'G' class Single in the Lewes area. The train includes a seven-compartment bogie 1st of 1880, the first bogie vehicles to be built for the LBSCR. Note the typical slotted post signal and attractive shaded lettering on the whistle board.
E. J. Bedford/M. J. Cruttenden Collection

Centre left: No 188 *Allen Sarle* on Lewes old curve on 7 June 1889. Note how leading van is down on springs, also the fine slotted bracket signal.
E. J. Bedford/M. J. Cruttenden Collection

Bottom left: A fine action shot of a 'Gladstone' emerging from Lewes tunnel with an Eastbourne-Victoria express. *E. J. Bedford/M. J. Cruttenden Collection*

Top: Another 'Gladstone' brings a southbound express into Haywards Heath. The photograph shows the December 1888 Pullman set with the leading Pullman Pup No 80 in original condition, with narrow vestibules, followed by two parlour cars, *Princess* and *Albert Victor* and the kitchen car *Prince*.
E. J. Bedford/M. J. Cruttenden Collection

Above: A 'D1' draws a rake of Stroudley carriages from Kingston tunnel, west of Lewes on the coast line in the 1880s. The heavily ballasted track is typical of the period and the bare appearance of the countryside unfamiliar to modern eyes. The thick afforestation of some lower parts of the Downs only dates from the late Victorian era.
E. J. Bedford/M. J. Cruttenden Collection

Engine 186, "De la Warr" on:—
The last train to cross old bridge Shoreham
ph: 8 June 1892

Above: 'Gladstone' class No 186 *De la Warr* takes the last down train across the old bridge over the River Adur at Shoreham on 8 June 1892.
E. J. Bedford/Bluebell Archives

Below: Royal Mail van No 402, one of three built to Diagram 48/223 in 1878. These vans were unique amongst Stroudley vehicles in having clerestory roofs, presumably to enable sorters to see more clearly what they were doing. They ran in conjunction with a six-wheel brake van modified by the removal of duckets and alterations to the doors. Photographed here as part of the 1882 official Lovers Walk series, the van survived until 1899. *LBSCR Official/Crown Copyright NRM York*

ROYAL   MAIL
402

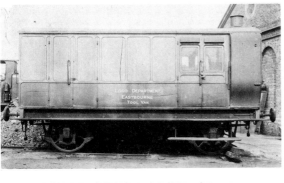

Above: For main line work Stroudley favoured a six-wheel design Diagram 37/44 for the 1st class. The unfortunate 2nd and 3rd passengers had to continue to make do with four-wheelers. No 539, one of a batch built in 1879 is in an attractive experimental livery of olive green with white upper panels which was amongst a number of schemes considered by the Directors in 1903 prior to the adoption of the umber and white livery. The use of the Company coat of arms was not perpetuated, other than on some saloons built the same year. *D. J. W. Brough Collection*

Centre left: A large number of 20ft full brakes were built between 1881 and 1891 to Diagram 47. Withdrawals began at the turn of the century and many became service vehicles. This one is in use as the Eastbourne shed tool van.
H. M. Madgwick Collection/IAL

Bottom left: Stroudley's horseboxes were tiny affairs. No 74 of Diagram 53/271 built in 1894 is a typical example. Note the limewash smears under the drop flap. One survivor lasted until 1956 on the Isle of Wight. On the left is the end of a passenger cattle wagon. *Lens of Sutton*

Top left: General 5 plank open merchandise wagon at Lovers Walk in 1882. Although probably painted up in a photographic livery, the wagon does clearly show lettering details. The illiterate symbol of a shield in a circle with the number in shaded letters below seems to have been in use until 1900. The A series comprised these high round ended wagons — this one has a chain to secure the tarpaulins but later a bar was used. The wagon was new when photographed and the type with changes to the buffing gear, brakes and axleguards remained the standard open until grouping.
LBSCR Official/Crown Copyright NRM York

Centre left: The standard covered van also continued through the years with few changes. The design looks very modern for 1882, when compared to its contemporaries on other railways. When fitted with a steel underframe, as many later examples were, it would not look out of place today..
LBSCR Official/Crown Copyright NRM York

Bottom left: Brake van No 57 was built June 1882 at a cost of £209 12s 9d. Stroudley's vans were of the road

van type with no verandahs and the earlier vehicles had lantern roofs. These were subsequently removed. Although the design was not perpetuated by Billinton, a number of vans lasted into Southern days, this one being withdrawn August 1924.
LBSCR Official/Crown Copyright NRM York

Top: Eight-ton van No 8205, a similar vehicle to 1577 but in the livery current c1903-10. Photographed at Lewes shortly after a repaint in 1907.
G. F. Burtt/Lens of Sutton

Above: The beginning of the end of the Stroudley era. No 602 *Goodwood* paired with a Craven tender instead of the Stroudley outside-framed one it had during its working life, one of the first of Stroudley's large 0-6-0s, 'C' class No 408 of 1871, and 0-4-2s Nos 609 *Devonshire* and 613 *Norfolk* await their last journey at Lovers Walk after sale for scrap to Moss Isaacs of Deptford Wharf in January 1902.
H. M. Madgwick Collection/IAL

The Robert Billinton Period

Above: 'D3' Class No 365 *Victoria* on the Lewes turntable in the 1890s. This was Robert Billinton's first class which emerged from Brighton works in 1892. Following a routine life in Brighton days, this locomotive made its mark on history when it brought down a German warplane over the Romney Marsh on 28 November 1942.
E. J. Bedford/M. J. Cruttenden Collection

Below: A superb photograph of 'D3' No 373 *Billingshurst* at Hove. The driver is James Wiltshire of New Cross shed ready to take a London based semi-fast back to base. The Midland influence at Brighton in the 1890s is apparent. *M. P. Bennett/Bluebell Archives*

Top: On taking over as Locomotive Superintendent, R. J. Billinton soon introduced locomotives with leading bogies that Stroudley had been unwilling to adopt. His first class of 4-4-0s was the 'B2', handsome looking locomotives that proved to be underboilered. J. N. Maskelyne said that they were 'all legs'. No 316 *Goldsmid* of 1895 and another member of the class wait to leave the smoky environs of London Bridge c1902. *M. P. Bennett/Bluebell Archives*

Above: *Goldsmid* was named after the Company's chairman but most 'B2s' were named after eminent engineers. No 319 *John Fowler* is raised up on massive wooden shearlegs at Fratton where many of the class were shedded. *K. Marx Collection*

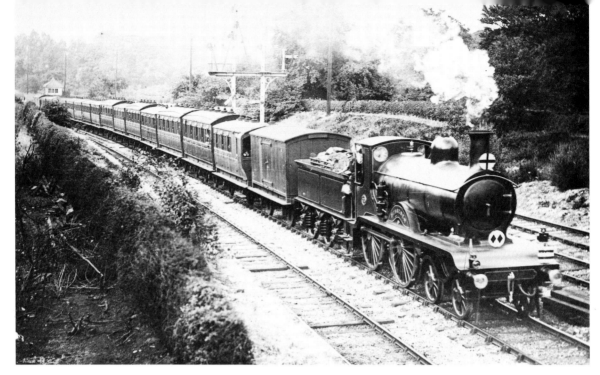

Top: Billinton appears to have realised his mistake and in 1897, the sole 'B3' No 213 *Bessemer* appeared, an intermediate step between the 'B2s' and 'B4s'. It is pictured here on a Victoria-Portsmouth train in a popular photographic location, the four track section by Balham Intermediate signalbox. The rolling stock consists of mixed Stroudley and Billinton stock, the higher pitched roofs of the latter being apparent. The first vehicle is the solitary bullion van to Diagram 79/230 built June 1899 which lasted into Southern days.
Dr T. F. Budden/LGRP (by kind permission of David & Charles Ltd)

Above: No 45 *Bessborough* of the highly successful 'B4' class at Lewes. This engine was fitted when new with a Drummond firebox. Note the casing for the Drummond cross water tubes, the only LBSCR locomotive to have these. The apparatus was removed at the beginning of 1912, the economies of this experiment shown to be negligible. *Lens of Sutton*

Above: An unusual cab view of a 'B4' at Lewes East signalbox. The driver, H. Aylwin and his fireman have on their caps the distinctive badges with 'D3' *Goldsmid* depicted on them. The polished oil cans gleam on a shelf in the centre. Under the cab roof below the driver's name is inscribed the customary mileage tally stating that from 2 November 1905 to 6 November 1907 the locomotive had run 55,730 miles. Henry Aylwin's locomotive was *Siemens* built in 1899, and later in September 1908 renamed to *Sussex*, the name taken from No 72 which happened to be in works over the same period! *IAL*

Below: For goods work, Billinton developed a Stroudley design and the 'E3' radial tanks were the result. No 457 *Watersfield* hauls a goods train through Norwood Junction c1905. Evocative enamel signs for BDV cigarettes and the Waverley pen appear in the background. The wagons are mainly private owner coal wagons with a LBSCR van at the head.
H. M. Madgwick Collection/IAL

Top left: The next development was the 'E4'. No 481 *Itchingfield* was one of the early members of the class painted in the goods green at first. The roof of the rebuilt Brighton station soars over the engine as it lets off steam. A Billinton six-wheel 2nd stands behind a well dressed lady who is sitting on one of the first LBSCR standard platform seats.
M. P. Bennett/Bluebell Archives

Centre left: The proportions of an 'E4' and the final development of the Billinton radial tank the 'E6' may be compared in this view at Eastbourne old shed of Nos 479 *Donnington* and 409 *Graffham* whose name is almost indistinguishable.
M. P. Bennett/Bluebell Archives

Bottom left: A welcome pause in shunting for the crew of 'Terrier' No 76 *Hailsham* at Polegate, certainly a novel use for the Stroudley tool box. For the first part of its career *Hailsham* was stationed at the town of that name, working the branch trains to Polegate, but in the 1880s was transferred to Eastbourne shed following the opening of the Cuckoo line.
M. P. Bennett/Bluebell Archives

Top: 'Terrier' No 63 *Preston* pauses at Kemp Town terminus in the course of running round its train. The passengers are making their way towards the exit as the points are changed. Kemp Town was not unlike a model railway layout — the tracks plunged straight out of the station into a lengthy single bore tunnel set in the chalk cliff. *M. P. Bennett/Bluebell Archives*

Above: 'Gladstone' No 198 *Sheffield* passing the Pullman car works at Preston Park with a train of Billinton stock c1903 including one vehicle in the experimental green and white livery. The lines on the right are those of the Cliftonville Spur built in 1879 to enable Worthing trains to avoid Brighton. The end coach in the siding next to the main line train curiously bears a discarded West Croydon nameboard upside down on its roof. *M. P. Bennett/Bluebell Archives*

Above: 'D' Class No 362 *Kidbrooke*, the last of the class to be built, on a line of dumb buffered Stephenson Clarke wagons at Hove, c1902. Stephenson Clarke held the locomotive coal contract for the LBSCR and their wagons were much in evidence. In the carriage sidings is a rake of Stroudley six-wheel firsts of Diagram 37/44. The board peeping under the footbridge proclaims Horace Saunders, formerly James Ireland & Co, Timber Merchant whose office and Central Yard here was linked to the Brighton Saw Mill in Church Street.
M. P. Bennett/Bluebell Archives

Centre right: 'Terrier' *Wapping* as No 671 between 1901 and 1905 at Portsmouth and Southsea in the process of shunting two very interesting vehicles. The four-wheeler is one of the bullion vans followed by one of the two Diagram 68/224 clerestory Royal Mail vans of 1897. Behind is an LBSCR cattle van of standard Stroudley pattern.
Rixon Bucknall Collection/IAL

Bottom right: No 116 *Touraine*, a Stroudley 'E1' reposes in a very unlikely spot, c1900. On the surface it would seem as though the driver has parked his engine and gone in for a drink in the local over the road. In fact the locomotive is out of service (one of the main connecting rods lies in the cab), parked at the end of a spur on the up side at the old Three Bridges station. When the line was widened, the Fox Inn was rebuilt further back. Surrounded by felled timber and with an old tree acting as a canopy, *Touraine* would appear to be in the depths of the country rather than a few yards from the Brighton main line.
O. J. Morris Collection/Lens of Sutton

Above: Aftermath of the Wivelsfield disaster of 23 December 1899. The remains of a 48ft ½in composite rest on a bogie. The construction of the carriages of the period is clearly revealed. Despite the destruction all around it the toilet roll holder remains intact! Beside the carriage is an ancient four wheeler from the breakdown train probably converted from a 3rd of the 1840s. *H. M. Madgwick Collection/IAL*

Below: A derailment in the country — location unknown. The open wagon 9205 is of the A type with steel underframe and shows the type of lettering favoured from c1903 to c1910. Beyond it a Billinton brake van hangs over the abutment of a bridge under the line. The Brighton appeared to have a suitably labelled tarpaulin available to seal on the spot the wagon's fate. *H. M. Madgwick Collection/IAL*

Above: A cartoon of Allen Sarle who with Samuel Laing largely guided the affairs of the Brighton company through the first half century with considerable flair. The two men's careers so closely parallel each other that a vital understanding between these two key office holders must have proved an essential factor in the success of the concern. Sarle joined the Company in 1848, worked his way through the audit office to become company accountant in 1854 and secretary in 1867. In 1885 this latter office was merged with that of general manager till his resignation in October 1897. His name will be distinctly familiar to any railway historian studying the numerous Company documents which bear his signature.
M. Joly Collection

Right: Samuel Laing began his career as a law clerk in the Railway Department of the Board of Trade and held office as chairman of the LBSCR between 1848 and 1855. After a period of service in India he was called back to take over the reins again as chairman after the financial collapse of 1867. Ranking among his major contributions are his rescue and rehabilitation of the Company and his discerning diplomacy in keeping other railway companies out of Brighton territory, thus laying the foundations for the prosperity of the later Victorian and Edwardian period. He was noted for the interest he took in his staff. He retired in 1896 and died the following year. Perhaps the finest tribute came from his opposite number on the rival South-Eastern, Sir George Russell, who said he regarded Mr Laing 'as possessed of the finest intellect and most cultivated mind of any man then left who was actively engaged in railway work'. *M. Joly Collection*

Right: The company's seal heads an invitation from the directors to meet the newly accoladed Sir Allen Sarle. *M. Joly Collection*

Below right: The menu and toast list of the annual railwaymen's dinner speaks for itself. Customary in those days was the vogue for solo songs, though it was not a case of singing for one's supper as the toasts followed the dinner. Mr Deakin appears to have been indisposed! The toast to the Stroudleys was symptomatic of the affection in which they were held by the railwaymen. *M. Joly Collection*

The Directors of
the London, Brighton and South Coast Railway Company
request the pleasure of

Company at Dinner at the Grand Hotel,
Northumberland Avenue, at 8 o'clock,
on Wednesday, July 1st 1896,
To meet Sir Allen Sarle.

*An early answer is requested, addressed to The Secretary,
Board Room, Brighton Co's Offices, London Bridge Terminus, S.E.*

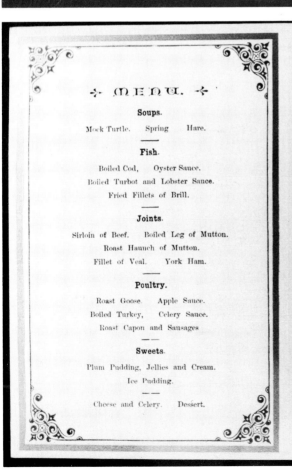

✦ MENU. ✦

Soups.

Mock Turtle.   Spring   Hare.

Fish.

Boiled Cod,   Oyster Sauce.
Boiled Turbot and Lobster Sauce.
Fried Fillets of Brill.

Joints.

Sirloin of Beef.   Boiled Leg of Mutton.
Roast Haunch of Mutton.
Fillet of Veal.   York Ham.

Poultry.

Roast Goose.   Apple Sauce.
Boiled Turkey,   Celery Sauce.
Roast Capon and Sausages

Sweets.

Plum Pudding, Jellies and Cream.
Ice Pudding.

Cheese and Celery.   Dessert.

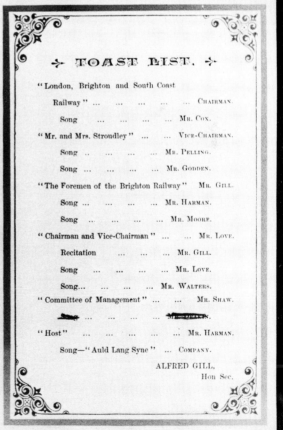

✦ TOAST LIST. ✦

"London, Brighton and South Coast
Railway" ... ... CHAIRMAN.
Song ... ... MR. COX.
"Mr. and Mrs. Stroudley" ... ... VICE-CHAIRMAN.
Song ... ... MR. PELLING.
Song ... ... MR. GODDEN.
"The Foremen of the Brighton Railway" MR. GILL.
Song ... ... MR. HARMAN.
Song ... ... MR. MOORE.
"Chairman and Vice-Chairman" ... ... MR. LOVE.
Recitation ... ... MR. GILL.
Song ... ... MR. LOVE.
Song... ... ... MR. WALTERS.
"Committee of Management" ... ... MR. SHAW.
̶ ̶ ̶ ... ... ̶ ̶ ̶.
"Host" ... ... MR. HARMAN.
Song—"Auld Lang Syne" ... COMPANY.

ALFRED GILL,
Hon Sec.

LONDON AND SOUTH WESTERN RAILWAY
AND
LONDON BRIGHTON AND SOUTH COAST RAILWAY.

Station Masters and Heads of Departments must see that a copy of this Notice is handed to every person who may be in any way engaged in connection with the working of the Train, including Signalmen, Crossing Keepers, Flagmen and Fogmen, who must read it carefully, and strictly act up to and obey the instructions contained therein. No want of knowledge of these instructions can be accepted as an excuse for any failure or neglect of duty.

TO THE OFFICERS AND SERVANTS OF THIS AND OTHER COMPANIES CONCERNED.

FUNERAL TRAIN CONVEYING THE
BODY OF HER LATE MAJESTY QUEEN VICTORIA,
Accompanied by the Chief Mourner,
H.M. KING EDWARD VII.
AND
H.I.M. THE GERMAN EMPEROR
AND THE OTHER ROYAL PRINCES,

On SATURDAY, FEBRUARY 2nd, 1901.

FROM GOSPORT (S.W.R.) TO VICTORIA (*via Fareham, Cosham, Havant, Ford Junction, Horsham, Dorking and Mitcham Junction*):—

TIME TABLE.

UP JOURNEY.	PILOT. A.M. arr.	pass.	dep.	ROYAL TRAIN. A.M. arr.	pass.	dep.	UP JOURNEY.	PILOT. A.M. arr.	pass.	dep.	ROYAL TRAIN. A.M. arr.	pass.	dep.
Gosport (Clarence Yard, S.W.R.)	...		8 35	...		8 45	Stammerham Junction			9 32			10 2
Gosport	8 38			8 48			Horsham			9 55			10 5
Fareham	...		8 48	8 54		8 58	Warnham			9 58			10 8
Cosham	8 57			9 7			Ockley			10 3			10 13
Farlington Junction	9 0			9 10			Holmwood			10 6			10 16
Havant Junction	9 5			9 15			Dorking			10 13			10 23
Bosham	9 11			9 21			Leatherhead Junction			10 18			10 28
Chichester	9 15			9 25			Epsom Junction			10 23			10 33
Drayton	9 17			9 27			Sutton Junction			10 28			10 38
Barnham Junction	9 22			9 32			Mitcham Junction			10 33			10 43
Ford Junction	9 26			9 36			Streatham Junction South			10 37			10 47
Arundel	9 30			9 40			Balham Junction (Main Line)			10 40			10 50
Amberley	9 34			9 44			Clapham Junction			10 44			10 54
Hardham Junction	9 39			9 49			Grosvenor Road (slowly)			10 48			10 58
Pulborough	9 40			9 50			Victoria			10 50	...	11 0	...
Billingshurst	9 46			9 56									

The Royal Train will consist of eight Vehicles.

On leaving Fareham, the Vehicles forming the Royal Train will run in the following order, viz. :—
Brake Van, Saloon, Funeral Car, Royal Saloon, Saloon, Bogie First, Bogie First and Brake Van.

The Pilot Engine and the Engine of the Royal Train will carry the following Head Signals.

Clear Weather :—Three White Boards with a Double Diamond painted on them, one on top of Smoke Box and one on each end of Buffer Beam.

Foggy Weather :—Four Lights. A Green Light on top of Smoke Box, a Green Light on centre of Buffer Beam, and a White Light on each end of Buffer Beam.

South Western Company's Engines and Guards will work the above Services from Gosport to Fareham.

Brighton Company's Engines and Guards will work forward from Fareham (S.W.R.) to Victoria, the Pilot and Royal Train being in charge of South Western Company's Pilotmen from Fareham (S.W.R.) to Farlington Junction.

Left: The end of an epoch — the working notice for Victoria's funeral train. Note the separate table for the customary pilot engine running 10 minutes ahead of the royal train. The working was shared with the LSWR which brought the specials as far as Fareham. There the Brighton men took over, but retained South Western pilotmen aboard as far as Farlington Junction over the jointly owned section. A twelve minute late start from Fareham was recovered to give a remarkable journey time from there to Victoria of 1hr 50min.
M. Joly Collection

Right: A beautifully produced luncheon card for Derby Day 1898 depicting a 'B2' on the cover. Featured in the menu was mayonnaise of salmon and lobster salad while the champagne was Pommery and Greno's 1889 Extra Sec. James Bradford was the catering contractor.   *D. J. W. Brough Collection*

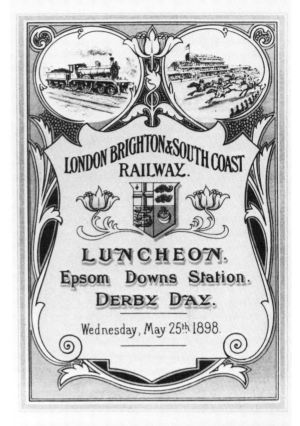

Bottom: 'Railway Jack' was the first and most famous precursor of a long line of dogs bearing, strapped on their backs, collecting boxes and soliciting the travelling public for contributions towards railway orphanages. The dog in this June 1881 picture was owned by station master Moore of Lewes and travelled by himself all around the system with a certain degree of help from station staff. He was much in demand at balls and dinners. He met with an unfortunate accident at Norwood Junction the following year in which he lost a leg, much to the consternation of the general public who followed the progress of his recovery with great interest. Many further Railway Jacks took up the cause, and a stuffed 'London Jack' may be seen in the Bluebell Railway Museum today.
From the Reeves Collection — reproduced by courtesy of the Sunday Times *and the Sussex Archeological Society*

Top right: A boy doffs his boater to men and officers of the French Navy being conveyed from Portsmouth to London in August 1905. The engine 'B4' No 54 *Empress*, renamed *La France* for the occasion celebrating the Entente Cordiale, is decorated in the best Brighton tradition. A rake of American Pullmans provide the train with a 'Pullman Pup' generator van for the electric lighting. The signalman watches from the elevated position of Horsham South signalbox which dated from the 1875 resignalling of the station. *H. M. Madgwick Collection/IAL*

Centre right: A resplendent 'B4' draws the 1897 royal train into Eastbourne station. The royal coat of arms (now at the National Railway Museum) and a crown are carried. Behind stands the old roundhouse and on the right Eastbourne signalbox, a large structure of timber on a brick base built in 1882 and still extant today. *M. P. Bennett/Bluebell Archives*

Below: The arrival of Henry, 15th Duke of Norfolk and his wife, the Hon Gwendolen Constable-Maxwell at Arundel in 1904 after their marriage. The troops provide a guard of honour while the prodigious amount of bunting flutters in the wind. The station staff at Arundel must have been well used to important personages passing through to their illustrious neighbours at the Castle. The station buildings of 1863 have changed little to this day, though they are no longer covered with ivy. The yard is well filled with carriages. *Courtesy R. Halls*

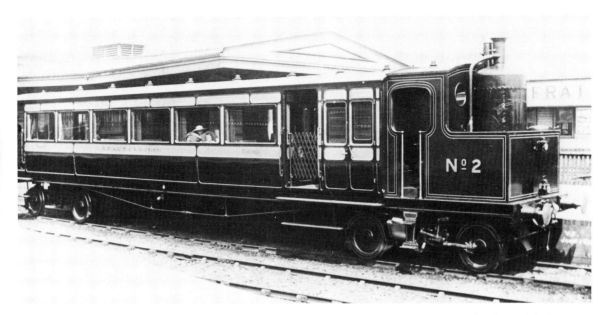

Above: To work the jointly owned East Southsea branch the LBSCR and LSWR built two railmotors. The second is seen here at Fratton immediately after entering service in June 1903. The vertical boilers were soon replaced and photographs of them in original condition are rare.
V. Chambers/J. R. Minnis Collection

Below: *The Arundel* is an example of one of the later American-style Pullman cars. Built in July 1899, it and its sister vehicle *The Chichester* were the first Pullmans in Britain to be fitted with six wheel bogies. The elaborate lining on the otherwise unadorned dark green livery is clearly seen. *The Arundel* was involved in the Wivelsfield accident but escaped unscathed to be rebuilt in 1905 as a kitchen car *Majestic* before final withdrawal in 1932. *D. J. W. Brough Collection*

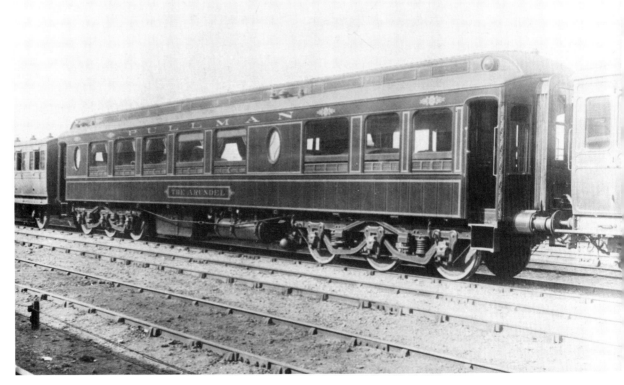

Above: The King's saloon No 562 to Diagram 85 in shops. A most imposing vehicle, it was the only LBSCR carriage other than the directors' saloon to be fitted on six-wheel bogies *D. J. W. Brough Collection*

Below: R. J. Billinton's horseboxes, while they retained a family resemblance to those of Stroudley, had a much steeper pitch to the roof and were considerably larger. No 291, one of the later examples built in 1903, was of the 18ft 6in variety to Diagram 81/272. *H. M. Madgwick Collection/IAL*

Top: The New Cross breakdown crane No 316S built in 1898 by Cowans, Sheldon stands in the old works yard at New Cross, on 14 September 1901. It had a sister based at Brighton. Behind is the rest of the train, comprising two very old Craven carriages soon to be replaced with Stroudley four wheelers and an Open Goods A with a tarpaulin marked Loco Dept, New Cross. The nearer coach has very square proportions and has suffered few alterations other than the blocking of most doorways and the fitting of a stove. Its precise identity is hard to determine but it is possibly an 1851 composite. A venerable relic is the whitewashed building known as the Croydon shed, dating back to 1845 which, though damaged in the last war, lasted until the 1950s.
Dr A. C. Hovenden/J. R. Minnis Collection

Above: Billinton's brake vans were the first the company had with verandahs, previously all were of the road van type. 10ton van No 29 built June 1897 photographed around 1905 in the livery of the day. One wonders whether Billinton brought his liking for large numbers on brake vans from the Midland where it was standard practice. Note the curious ampersand favoured by the LB&SCR.
Lens of Sutton

Above: Arundel goods yard c1908 with the town and castle in the background. This view gives a very good idea of the vehicles to be found in a goods yard on the LBSCR. There are 19 opens and three vans reflecting the proportions of the types found nationally. Secondly, the stock is all of common types — specialised wagons were rare. Most of the 16 LBSCR wagons are Open Goods A's. Note how most loads are covered by tarpaulins. There are also two vans and an Open D. Other companies stock includes one GNR open, one GER van and two MR coal wagons, the most numerous type of wagon in the country and to be found in almost every LBSCR yard. Two private owner wagons from Cannock Chase and Mapperley Collieries have brought coal to the town. *H. M. Madgwick Collection/IAL*

Below: An early 20th century version of containerisation probably taken at Fratton, since the containers belong to a Portsmouth firm. The LBSCR was using machinery trucks, the only number visible being 7160, for this traffic. Sandwiched between them is an ex-LCDR flat wagon marked 'For Highway Vehicles'. Removal companies were extensive users of containers from quite early days, the size being dictated by the road drays available. *H. M. Madgwick Collection/IAL*

Below: Willow Walk, adjacent to the SER establishment at Bricklayers Arms was the LBSCR's main goods depot in London. In this 1903 picture, the hydraulic crane is unloading from a dray massive tree trunks which will be conveyed by bolster wagon. Two Open Goods A loaded to a great height with hay and an Open Goods D are the wagons visible. The latter and one of the Open As are in the shortlived lettering style of LB&SC R^Y while the other bears the usual LB&SCR that followed.
C. W. Underhill Collection

Bottom: Another scene at Willow Walk the same year. Barrels being loaded on to one of the company's drays outside the Continental shed. Packaging in this period usually took the form of barrels, sacks and wicker baskets. The beautiful lettering on the dray is in a face not used elsewhere by the company and probably the work of an independent sign writer.
C. W. Underhill Collection

Above: The Erecting Shop, Brighton Works with Gladstone 197 *Jonas Levy* followed by 'B2' No 209 *Wolfe Barry*. In between the lines of locomotives stands a most impressive array of wheels.
M. P. Bennett/Bluebell Archives

Centre right: Another view further down the Erecting Shop, showing 'C' class No 411 and 'E1' No 115 *Lorraine* in the foreground with another 'C' in the far line.
H. M. Madgwick Collection/IAL

Bottom right: The Boiler Shop with the Erecting Shop in the distance in 1905.
H. M. Madgwick Collection/IAL

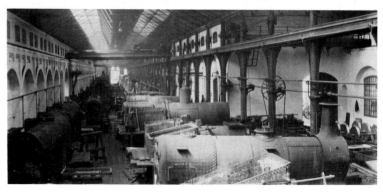

Above: Brighton Works always carried out a certain amount of scrapping on the premises. In the centre of the complex stood the small scrapyard which received dismantled components of rolling stock which after further cutting up were dispatched on to the wagons standing on the right. *H. M. Madgwick Collection/IAL*

Below: About 200 double bolster timber trucks were built to Drawing 2653/17 from 1899 onwards. As may be seen, their loads were by no means restricted to timber. This pair Nos 7761 and 4042 are standing in a corner of Brighton Works yard loaded with boilers. *G. F. Burtt/IAL*

Above: The carriage shops at Brighton with a number of Billinton bogie carriages and a horsebox under construction. An American Pullman receives attention on the right. With the exception of the underframe in the centre, all the construction visible is in wood, including the upturned six-wheeler underframe.
H. M. Madgwick Collection/IAL

Below: Inside the Brighton Paint Shop in 1903 a number of vehicles receive their first applications of the newly introduced umber and white livery. The clerestory roofed six wheeler in the centre is one of the four very handsome saloons built that year. Behind it stands one of the coaches of the royal train. Note the gas jets suspended from the roof used for lighting.
M. Joly Collection

Below: The LBSCR established its signal works at Coldblow, a little to the north of New Cross in 1849. Sandwiched between the main line and the Deptford Wharf branch, they remained in use until 1928. O. J. Morris took this picture a year later. Coldblow Crossing spans the Deptford Wharf line before it swings sharply round to the right to pass under the main line which is visible in the background. Behind the curve is a sight of the old Surrey Canal, now filled in.
O. J. Morris/Lens of Sutton

Bottom: The Grosvenor Hotel dwarfs the ramshackle wooden buildings of the original Victoria station. The gates and railings to the station yard were common practice with the company's larger stations. When the station was rebuilt, the thrifty management had part of the elaborate porte-cochère re-erected at Hove.
Lens of Sutton

VICTORIA STATION.   (LB & SCR)

Above: Providing a contrast with the previous picture is the new station completed in 1907/08. The unique feature of it was that it was in effect two stations joined end to end. *D. J. W. Brough Collection*

Below: The City terminus, London Bridge was for many years regarded as the principal one. The smoky atmosphere is beautifully captured in this c1904 view. Trains in the platforms include two 'Gladstones' on expresses and a 'D1' and two Billinton radial tanks on suburban trains. *H. M. Madgwick Collection/IAL*

2744. LONDON BRIDGE.

Top left: Work is commencing on widening the lines through Wandsworth Common in 1907. The new up main platform is under construction but the old island platform has not yet received attention. The signalbox soon to be replaced is of the standard pattern introduced in 1876 and is mounted on massive timbers reinforced with cast iron brackets over the up main. *H. M. Madgwick Collection/IAL*

Centre left: Thornton Heath had been rebuilt a few years earlier in 1903 when a new station building was constructed on the road overbridge. The building has the spacious quality characteristic of the later years of the company's existence. The valancing on the awning, similar to the SER pattern but smaller, was used on occasions. The pretty cupola and circular windows lighting the booking hall are noteworthy. One of the railway's competitors, a Croydon Corporation Tramways car passes. *Lens of Sutton*

Below: The original buildings of 1865 during rebuilding at Selhurst c1903. To judge from the state of the building, rebuilding came none too soon. Work is well advanced for the supports for the new awnings are erected and the subway constructed. The platform has been rebuilt in brick — it formerly consisted of wooden planks. *L. E. Brailsford/Lens of Sutton*

Below: Looking south from East Croydon c1900 with the South signalbox of 1897 in the centre. To the right is Fairfield yard which originally formed part of the Central Croydon branch. This had a very chequered career, finally being closed in 1890. The station site was used for building the Town Hall and the remainder kept as sidings. Waiting for its return journey to north London is a Webb 2-4-2T of the LNWR, one of the many forgotten through services that used to operate in London. East Croydon had quite a cosmopolitan flavour with the LNWR and GER as regular visitors as well as, of course, the SECR. *Dr A. C. Hovenden/IAL*

Bottom: East Croydon c1910 showing the range of buildings erected in 1895 in an elaborate if not particularly attractive style. The building is little altered today except for the removal of the lantern roofs. *Lens of Sutton*

68

Above: The South London line connecting London Bridge and Victoria was perhaps one of the nearest things in this country to an American elevated railway. For much of its length, the line straddled viaducts high above the teeming inner suburbs. Queens Road, Peckham was a typical station with its flimsy wooden buildings just off a main road. To meet the stiff competition provided by the LCC tramways, the line was electrified in 1909 and the new services were promoted under the name 'Elevated Electric'. Blue plates bearing this name were erected at each station. *W. H. Smith & Sons/Lens of Sutton*

Below: Streatham in the 1890s before a new booking office was erected on the bridge c1900. In its original 1868 form shown here, it had ridge and furrow type awnings with elaborate valancing similar to that on the South London line. They were replaced with the familiar 'loping' design, along with similar structures at Mitcham Junction and Hackbridge. Streatham was then very much an outer suburb with large villas in their own grounds. *Lens of Sutton*

Above: One of the more unsavoury parts of the system was the East London line with its tunnel under the Thames through which the 'Terriers' poured forth their sulphureous fumes. The East London Railway in which the LBSCR maintained a substantial interest had its own station at New Cross on the east side of the existing premises. This picture of 18 July 1898 depicts the melancholy scene after closure with weeds growing on the platforms and track, nameboard part dismantled and lamps 'beheaded'. While of indifferent quality, it is the only known photograph of the separate East London station. *NRM, Crown Copyright*

Below: East Dulwich c1910 showing the station building erected in 1868. A competitive London bound tram is about to pass under the plain but none the less attractive bridge into the still rural surrounds of Dog Kennel Hill. *D. J. W. Brough Collection*

Above: The Crystal Palace was a source of much traffic to the LBSCR and indeed it was built on land belonging to Leo Schuster, a director of the LBSCR who promoted its construction with Samuel Laing, who was Chairman of both the LBSCR and the Crystal Palace company. To serve it, a truly opulent station was opened in 1854. This is the only photograph that has come to light showing the original overall roof, dismantled before the Charing Cross roof collapse in 1905. Beyond it is the commodious station building equipped with refreshment rooms. *Lens of Sutton*

Centre left: This Arcadian scene is in fact in the London outer suburbs. Open A wagon No 10369 is standing at the end of the ballast sidings at Mitcham Junction in 1905. The siding seems to disappear into the hedgerows. *C. Steptoe/M. Joly Collection*

Bottom left: What surely must have been the tallest signals on the Brighton system frame Three Bridges station in 1903 prior to the line widening. The overall roofs were an unusual feature. That on the down side survives in part together with Mocatta's station building. The small locomotive shed was rebuilt on a much larger scale in 1909 further away from the station, when its site was taken for the widened lines. On the right is the small timber goods shed, typical of many erected by the company where traffic did not justify one of the usual brick structures spanning the track. *Lens of Sutton*

Above: Cabs leaving Brighton station c1903 with the heavy iron and glass porte cochère of 1882/3 prominent in the background. A stout constable intently studies a notice pinned to the gateposts.
H. M. Madgwick Collection/IAL

Below: Angmering, looking very spick and span after a repaint in c1908. The view, taken towards Ford, is of interest in that it shows clearly the painting styles in use. The station buildings date from the 1860s and the signalbox from 1877. On the platform is one of the two most common varieties of LBSCR seat, and flower baskets hang from the awning.
H. M. Madgwick Collection/IAL

Top: Bognor's station seemed to be ill-fated. First, it blew down in 1897, the resulting damage being shown here and then two years later, the main building at the head of the platform was almost completely destroyed by fire, only the chimneys and part of the west side of the building remaining standing.
H. M. Madgwick Collection/IAL

Above: After the fire, the company took the opportunity to build a magnificent new station. The extensive awnings with the distinctive 'loping' bargeboards favoured after 1898 and the turret are clearly visible in this picture of 1902 taken immediately after the new station opened. Standing in the platform is a very characteristic train of the type provided for secondary services, comprising Stroudley 'D' class No 228 *Seaford* and a six-coach set of Stroudley four-wheelers including two full brakes of Diagram 47, two 3rds and two four compartment composites or 1sts.
O. J. Morris Collection/Lens of Sutton

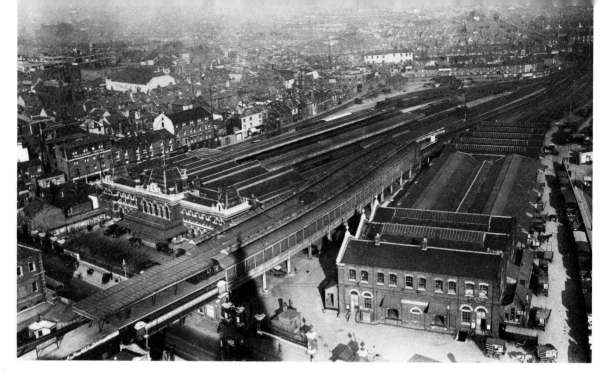

Top: Portsmouth & Southsea in 1931, the most recent photograph in the book, though the station was unchanged from pre-Group days. A joint station with the LSWR, it is pure LBSCR in its detail. The elaborate station buildings with their mansard roofs in the French Second Empire style were the height of fashion when built in the 1860s. In the centre we have the island platform of the high level of the station leading to Portsmouth Harbour and to the right the goods station replaced in 1936 by carriage sidings.
O. J. Morris Collection

Above: Portsmouth Harbour from which the steam packets crossed to the Isle of Wight. The station was suspended over the harbour on a jetty. Visitors must have had a fine view of the Imperial Fleet.
Lens of Sutton

Above: The rather attractive 'Swiss Chalet' station at Lewes had been replaced in 1889 by the present structure on a slightly different site. The original curve which became the goods avoiding line is seen diverging to the left. In this view 'B4' No 42 *His Majesty* is awaiting the rightaway with a London express in 1909. Note the lantern roof over the booking hall, a feature of which the company was especially fond in the 1880s. *M. P. Bennett/Bluebell Archives*

Below: Lewes, looking in the opposite direction at the same period with another 'B4' at the down London platform. A carriage truck, complete with carriage stands at the rear of an up train while 'D' class No 265 *Charlwood* heads a local train in the Barcombe direction. With its awnings and great glass roof in the angle of the junction, Lewes was an enormous station for the size of the town. It was due to its position as a focal point for railways in East Sussex that it derived its importance as a junction, a point made clear by the station nameboards with their instructions for changing trains. *Lens of Sutton*

Top left: Uckfield, dating from 1901, is a good example of the station rebuilds the company carried out at the turn of the century. The half timbering on the gables, applied in a form common to large houses of the period appears to be in recognition of the Wealden location at Uckfield. Awnings by this time were largely of steel as opposed to the wood of earlier years. The large number of staff employed is noteworthy and as if to counteract their rather self conscious posing for the photographer, the almost obligatory small boys have managed to get in the picture. The goods shed in the background is of typical design with iron framed semi-circular windows. *H. M. Madgwick Collection/IAL*

Bottom left: An everyday scene at Barnes Green Crossing, between Itchingfield Junction and Billingshurst. The LBSCR had more than its fair share of level crossings. Here the lady crossing keeper opens the gates to let a pony and trap through on 1 September 1910. *M. Joly Collection*

Top: Stroudley's marine masterpiece, the ss *Paris* of 1888 reposes at Newhaven, next to the enormous sheerlegs of the marine department. The large building behind is the company's marine workshops and beyond it are the twin gables of Newhaven locomotive shed. *M. Joly Collection*

Above: Further down the quay stands the ss *Arundel* built by Denny Bros in 1900. On the quayside tracks stands a four wheel meat van and a Grande Vitesse van. Beyond are the attractive buildings of the 1884 Newhaven Harbour station, the engaging little turrets showing an affinity to those at East Grinstead. *G. F. Burtt/IAL*

Above: 'Engineers Department No 2', a steam roller
built by Wallis & Stevens Ltd of Basingstoke and
purchased by the LBSCR on 9 October 1901. It was
withdrawn sometime after 1922 and sold to Shoreham
UDC who later re-sold to a Chichester contractor who
owned it at the time the photograph was taken.
H. M. Madgwick Collection/IAL

Right: In the 19th century, the suburban trains of the
LBSCR were not known for their punctuality or speed.
A childrens book by Edith Nesbit of 1906 incorporating
an 1899 drawing by H. R. Millar provides an
interesting contemporary reflection on the company's poor
reputation. Above a bridge, similar to those on the South
London line, protrudes an unmistakable Stroudley profile
while the advertisement draws the traveller's attention
to the dubious merits of frequent trains throughout the
year and the longest route to London Bridge via Tulse
Hill. *J. R. Minnis Collection*

Illustration to " The Bouncing Ball," in " Nine Unlikely
Tales for Children."

Above: A porter in a typical studio portrait. The setting with its back cloth showing a Venetian window is a little incongruous. The reverse indicates a studio in the Balham/Streatham area and conveys greetings to relations by the name of Boxall. *K. Marx Collection*

Above: A guard displays his handsome uniform.
D. J. W. Brough Collection

The Marsh Régime

Above: The Marsh era in evidence. Two of the larger new Atlantics, No 39 nearest the camera, receive attention in the erecting shop of Brighton Works. The five 'H1s' were delivered new from Kitsons between December 1905 and February 1906. The photograph probably portrays the first major overhaul at Brighton.
M. P. Bennett/Bluebell Archives

Right: 'H1' No 38 rushes through the chalk cuttings of the South Downs at Patcham with a train composed, apart from the Pullman car, of Marsh's elliptical roof stock in the beautiful but shortlived umber and white livery.
M. P. Bennett/Bluebell Archives

Left: The Brighton main line runs straight as a die for much of its length as is clearly seen here. No 41 hurries the down Pullman Limited beneath the high Ashenground bridge just south of Haywards Heath. The thickly wooded land bordering the track is the remains of the old forest that covered much of the High Weald and contrasts with the bare downland further south.
M. P. Bennett/Bluebell Archives

Below: Marsh's first design of tank locomotive, the 'I1' was unsuccessful, mainly because of the very small boiler. No 3 hauls a local comprising four Billinton six wheelers in the two tone livery into Hove from the west past some of the usual goods opens and a Stroudley brake No 137. Note the steps whitened for safety reasons.
M. P. Bennett/Bluebell Archives

Bottom: 'I2' No 13 leaves Hassocks on a wintry day. The four coach set is rebuilt from Billinton six-wheel stock. *H. Gordon Tidey/IAL*

Above: Sister locomotive No 12 waits at Addison Road, Kensington in 1926. A handsome design, though still underboilered. The vintage Lyons Ice Cream vans have probably come from nearby Cadby Hall.
O. J. Morris/IAL

Below: Marsh finally achieved success with his third 4-4-2T class, the 'I3'. True express engines and a match for the celebrated LNWR 'Precursors', they handled the back bone of main line traffic for many years. One of their duties was the through train to Brighton and Eastbourne, the 'Sunny South Express', introduced in 1905. No 87 is attached to a rake of LNWR stock at Addison Road. *Courtesy H. R. H. Wood*

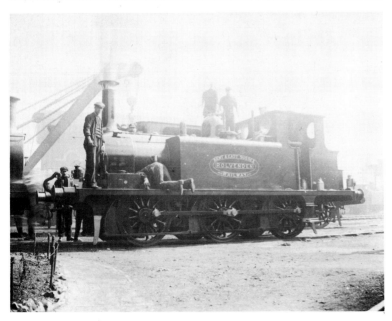

Above: Another Marsh 4-4-2T design that was rather less than successful was the 'I4', a superheated version of the 'I2'. No 33 hauls an Eastbourne excursion towards Southerham Junction.
M. P. Bennett/Bluebell Archives

Centre left: The first 'C3', No 300 of 1906, is shunted from the paint shop to the running shed at Brighton by 'E' class tank No 159 *Edenbridge*. The sheen of the lined black goods livery contrasts with the dull black used on the smokebox.
M. P. Bennett/Bluebell Archives

Bottom left: Maurice Bennett was very fortunate to capture this unique picture of Kent & East Sussex Railway, *Rolvenden* formerly No 71 *Wapping* at Brighton. The 'Terrier' was sold to the KESR in January 1905, and given its new livery at Brighton before departure to new pastures.
M. P. Bennett/Bluebell Archives

Top: 'Terrier' No 638 (formerly *Millwall*) came back from the dead, having supplied steam at Epsom in 1896-7 and then moved on to pumping duties at Three Bridges till towed away to shops in October 1905. This was most unusual, since engines relegated to stationary activities almost invariably ended in the scrapyard. When returned to traffic in August 1906, No 638 had been fitted with new cylinders and firebox and wooden numberplates while the tank sides were lettered 'Loco Dept' and the livery changed to black with red lining. It soldiered on until sold to the Admiralty in 1918 for use at Invergordon and survived a Government surplus sale to end up in 1923 as No 8 *Dido* on the Shropshire & Montgomery Railway to serve a further decade. Such was the resilience and ability of the Stroudley 'Terriers'.

In the photograph, taken at the Brighton Works yard by his brother, is Maurice Bennett himself on the cab steps. *Bluebell Archives*

Above: Extensive use was made of motor trains on both the east and west coast lines. As originally formed the trains consisted of a 'Terrier' and one elliptical roof auto coach, known as a 'Balloon' from the roof profile. These were sometimes run in pairs as in this picture of No 642 (formerly *Tulsehill*) with the West Worthing motor train. It is receiving some attention at the front end entering Shoreham-by-Sea from the east. The neat crossing keeper's house with its stuccoed walls is a common sight in Sussex.
M. P. Bennett/Bluebell Archives

Above: To haul the increasing number of motor trains Marsh started to rebuild the elderly 'Terriers'. No 677, old *Wonersh*, stands outside the locomotive shed at Tunbridge Wells, to which the engine was allocated. *W. G. Tilling/Bluebell Archives*

Below: Entering Epsom on a Victoria-Portsmouth stopping train in the spring of 1909, 'E5' class No 575 *Westergate*, passes a 'D' class tank waiting with the stock of a returning local to London. The 'E5' is running as a 2-4-2T, being one of 20 converted by Marsh from 0-6-2T by removal of the leading coupling rod sections. Marsh had arrived from Doncaster with an acute dislike of using front coupled tank engines on secondary services. By September 1909, however, all 20 had reverted to their former wheel arrangement. *M. P. Bennett/Bluebell Archives*

Top right: 'D' No 290 *Denbies* in umber hauls the 6.50 train to Haywards Heath which is formed of a main line elliptical roof set past Preston chalk banks in the cutting north of Preston Park station which is being widened to allow additional carriage sidings to be laid. The work of chipping away the chalk appears to be done entirely by hand. The long line of ballast trucks, which are of the most primitive type with their dumb buffers, has been commandeered to remove the chalk. Note the canvas covers to keep the ballast out of the axleboxes, and the livery style with BALLAST written along the top plank of each vehicle.
M. P. Bennett/Bluebell Archives

Centre right: 'D3' No 381 *Fittleworth*, still immaculate in its ochre livery, heads a local of mixed Stroudley and Billinton stock along the flat coastal plain. Portslade station is in the background. While the area is still largely rural, housing developments are already covering the fields to the south. By World War 1, most of the land as far west as Shoreham was built up.
M. P. Bennett/Bluebell Archives

Below: To the north of Patcham tunnel, No 199 *Samuel Laing* heads a set of elliptical roof stock. The distant signal displays the LBSCR practice of painting the arm red with a white stripe.
M. P. Bennett/Bluebell Archives

Above left: An unusual view of the footplate of 'B1' No 198 in Marsh umber at Brighton Works.
H. M. Madgwick Collection/IAL

Above right: The underboilered 'B2s' were rebuilt into very handsome maids of all work. No 321 poses at Eastbourne for an official photograph in 1907.
G. F. Burtt/IAL

Below: No 430 of Class C1 photographed c1911 at Coulsdon shed, opened in 1900 and closed in 1928. Based on the previous 'C' class, it appeared in the final batch of 1887 and was a Battersea engine. Only two of the dozen survived till the war during which No 430 put in sterling service hauling goods off the LNWR from Lillie Bridge, and even working a troop special as far north as Peterborough, and survived as the last member of the class on the Brighton until September 1924. Fellow survivor No 428 was sold to the Stratford on Avon & Midland Junction Railway in 1920. This photograph shows up the very distinctive ground signals of the Brighton known as 'Tommydods' or 'dummies'.
J. R. Minnis Collection

Above: 'B1' No 177 at East Croydon soon after its repaint to Marsh livery and bearing the new and decorative company monogram on the central splasher. *J. R. Minnis Collection*

Below: 'B1' No 187 receiving some attention up front as it draws into Lewes from London passing the Lewes West box of 1888 where signalman Ager stands on duty. *M. P. Bennett/Bluebell Archives*

Top: H. Gordon Tidey lived at Honor Oak Park and took many pictures in the cutting from the up platform at Honor Oak Park station. One such is 'B2X' No 317 complete with indicator shelter. The first vehicle is a Billinton five-compartment 3rd which is then followed by an elliptical roof set, with a Diagram 121/190 brake 3rd leading. The up starter signal is a good example of the standard Acfield design introduced c1900.
H. Gordon Tidey/J. R. Minnis Collection

Above: In one of the most beautiful of all LBSCR train photographs, a 'B2X' approaches Arundel station from the north with a South Coast express. The lovely evening light shines across the water meadows of the River Arun. *M. P. Bennett/Bluebell Archives*

Below: An elegantly composed view of 'D1' No 269 on a Brighton train passing an occupation crossing to the south of Steyning station.
M. P. Bennett/Bluebell Archives

Bottom: On the same visit 'D1' No 297 is captured entering Steyning from the south, shortly after resuming passenger duties in 1906 following a spell as paint shop pilot at Brighton and losing the name *Bonchurch* on going through works. The train consists of Stroudley four wheelers except for the leading luggage van which is one of the 34 Billinton double-ended vans built to Diagram 77/228 between 1894 and 1903. One facet of the Edwardian countryside often overlooked today is that there were few controls on advertising and hoardings. 'Advertising stations', as they were known, were put in the most rural locations. It is interesting to note that most of the products advertised are still available.
M. P. Bennett/Bluebell Archives

Above: Again taken the same day and from only a little further down the line is 'D3' No 373 (formerly *Billingshurst*) rounding a curve out of Bramber station with a train for Horsham. Note the neat appearance of the permanent way and of the grass verges.
M. P. Bennett/Bluebell Archives

Below: The same locomotive on another branch. 'D3' No 373 pauses at Barcombe's fine domestic revival station with an up stopping train to East Grinstead. Unusually it carries no headcode and boasts a battery of lamps above the side tank.
H. M. Madgwick Collection/IAL

Top: The pleasant rural surroundings of Hurst Green Junction make a splendid setting for an 'E5' coming off the East Grinstead line. *Lens of Sutton*

Above: A Brighton scene captured to prewar perfection as a down local enters Amberley in 1914, hauled by 'D1' No 268 and a rake of Billinton carriages constituting Set Train No 56.
O. J. Morris/D. J. W. Brough Collection

Above: An architectural feature of the main line regarded as one of the most delightful follies in England is the north portal of Clayton tunnel. 'B4' No 44 *Cecil Rhodes* draws out in this c1906 photograph. Many theories have been advanced as to the reasons for the design of the portal ranging from its possible use in an invasion to its reassuring the passenger for the long dark journey ahead. Certainly the addition of a cottage on the top c1850 was a stroke of genius by a man who had an eye, perhaps unconscious, for the picturesque. *M. P. Bennett/Bluebell Archives*

Below: As part of his rebuilding programme, Marsh tackled the Billinton 'C2' class. One of the resultant 'C2X' class No 448 is seen on the Quarry line near Redhill in 1922. A preponderance of private owner coal wagons is evident in the train.
O. J. Morris/J. R. Minnis Collection

Train Collision at East Croydon. July 10th 1909.

Bender & Lewis, Croydon.

Above: An extremely destructive accident at East Croydon on 10 July 1909 when 'I2' No 19 hauling an excursion collided with 'E5' No 572 *Farncombe* whilst piloting. Note the crowds on the station platform.
Bender & Lewis/K. Marx Collection

Left: The excursion engine in a sorry state at Brighton with damaged components held together by pieces of stout rope. Although the buffer beam and coupling has completely disappeared the bogie appears quite undamaged. In fact, No 19's bogie was cracked in the accident and the bogie, or pony truck as it was known to railwaymen, of sister engine No 13 was utilised to bring her to Brighton. *M. P. Bennett/Bluebell Archives*

Above right: During Marsh's regime at Brighton, the works became increasingly less capable of handling the number of general overhauls required. Many locomotives were stored at Horsted Keynes awaiting scrapping or repair and others on the Ashurst spur which, although opened in 1888, was not yet in regular use. A forlorn line of engines stand in the midst of the Sussex countryside c1907. They include 'E1' No 146 *Havre*, 'E4' No 516 *Rustington*, 'B4' No 51 *Wolferton*, 'E4' No 476 *Beeding*, 'E4' No 487 *Newick*, a 'C1', an 'E4' and two more 'B4s'.
H. M. Madgwick Collection/IAL

Right: To relieve congestion, the carriage and wagon works were moved to a new site at Lancing in 1909. The new works occupied a wide area for the company purchased enough land for future expansion. Two grounded bodies of a Stroudley Brake 3rd and a covered carriage truck to Diagram 82/253 stand beside the approach road soon after opening.
D. J. W. Brough Collection

L.B.&.SC.R. Carriage Works. Lancing.

Above: Testing a new coupling at Lancing Works. The two merchandise wagons bear the large lettering introduced c1913, that on the right being renumbered into the duplicate series. A similar wagon was still to be seen in this livery at Lancing in the mid-1930s.
M. Joly Collection

Right: The Brighton became one of the most prominent slip-coach operators in Britain, especially prior to 1914, and although slipping coaches was a frequent occurrence, it was rarely photographed. The Worthing portion of a train bound for Brighton has just been slipped at Preston Park and is gliding towards the station. The photograph interestingly shows the outcome and layout of sidings resulting from the hard manual labour of those employed in widening the cutting.
H. M. Madgwick Collection/IAL

Top: The distinctive lines of Marsh semi-elliptical stock are shown to advantage in this picture of the first run of Set Train No 50 behind 'D3' No 374 at Lewes on 4 July 1907. Lavatory brake 3rd No 719 of Diagram 121/190 is the first vehicle, followed by a third of Diagram 111/185 and a lavatory 1st of Diagram 124/61. The water crane of 1882 is a standard Stroudley design and lasted until the 1970s. Examples can still be seen on the Bluebell Railway today.
H. M. Madgwick Collection/IAL

Above: In 1907 LBSCR commenced the rebuilding of many of the comparatively new Billinton six-wheel carriages into bogie vehicles on new underframes. No 417, a five-compartment brake 3rd, was rebuilt in June 1907 from a five-compartment 3rd of 1895.
D. J. W. Brough Collection

Above: Perhaps the quaintest vehicles possessed by the company were a number of inspection cars which were little more than motor cars on flanged wheels. One is seen here in action on the main line. The attitude of the driver, who seems to be trying to extract more speed out of the contraption, contrasts with the phlegmatic expression of his passenger. The use of the usual headcode discs and lamps makes the whole thing look even stranger. *H. M. Madgwick Collection/IAL*

Right: An 'I4', No 35, makes an appropriate heading to a memorial to Mrs George Gates, founder of the Brighton Railway Mission. The Victorian moralists, particularly well-meaning ladies of the upper classes regarded the disreputable British navvy and his successors the railway staff as particularly unregenerate and therefore a worthy cause of charitable evangelism, and permanent missions were soon established in major railway centres. *K. Marx Collection*

THIS TABLET WAS ERECTED BY THE
FRIENDS OF THE RAILWAY MISSION
AND MEMBERS OF HER FAMILY.
IN LOVING MEMORY OF
MRS GEORGE GATES,
FOUNDER AND PRESIDENT OF THE
BRIGHTON RAILWAY MISSION.
WHO WAS CALLED TO HIGHER SERVICE
JULY 23RD 1911 HAVING PERSONALLY &
CONTINUOUSLY SUPERINTENDED THE
WORK FOR OVER 35 YEARS.
HER IMPLICIT AND UNWAVERING TRUST
IN GOD'S HOLY WORD, HER SINGLENESS
OF PURPOSE AND UNCEASING DEVOTION
TO THE WORK OF WINNING RAILWAY-
MEN TO JESUS CHRIST, BOTH IN THEIR
HOMES AND ALSO AT THE MISSION
HALL, HAVE WON FOR HER THE TITLE,
SO RICHLY DESERVED,
"THE RAILWAYMEN'S FRIEND"

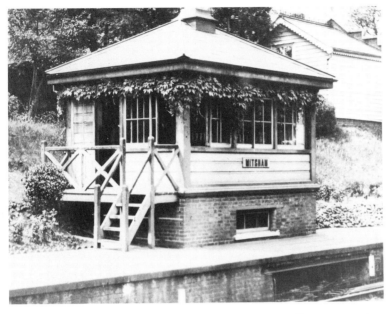

Top left: Mitcham, a small box which is still extant today, though sadly lacking the luxuriant growth of ivy that festooned it in 1908. The date of construction of the box is not known, but it probably dates from the 1890s. The Brighton practice of using small name boards with cut out wooden letters is clearly shown.
M. Joly Collection

Centre left: Windmill Bridge Junction, a Saxby & Farmer style box dating from 1878 and controlling the junction between the Victoria and London Bridge lines. Photographed in 1921, the box lasted until replaced under the Croydon area resignalling in 1954.
M. Joly Collection

Below: A posed official picture of one of the original three-coach South London sets with motor car No 3203 leading. Within a year the accommodation provided by the stock was found to be over lavish for the service and the first class centre trailer vehicle was converted to steam stock, while the motor coaches were reformed with new trailers.
D. J. W. Brough Collection

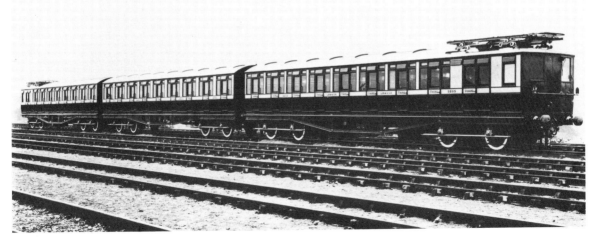

Right: The original electric sets built for the South London line had unusual seating arrangements, appearing externally to be conventional compartment vehicles but having side corridors. The example shown is one of the sumptous 1st class trailers.
NRM, Crown Copyright

Below: To serve the initial part of the LBSCR's electrification scheme, car sheds were built at Peckham in the space between the junction of the South London and Tulse Hill lines. They lacked any architectural pretensions being large ugly barns of corrugated iron. One of the original three-coach sets is beside the shed while one of the petrol electric railcars of 1905 No 4 stands in front. It had recently been converted to a maintenance vehicle as Electrical Department No 4   *Lens of Sutton*

Above: Cable laying operations for the expansion of the overhead electric at West Norwood. The station had been rebuilt with new platform awnings and a new signalbox erected in 1892.
M. Joly Collection

Below: Rolling stock for the later Crystal Palace scheme was of a more conventional pattern. A motor 3rd 3328 leads a train outside Streatham Hill station with the signalbox of 1898 on the left. *M. Joly Collection*

The Lawson Billinton Swansong

Above: The outdoor running staff with Col L. B. Billinton in the centre wearing spats. Marsh Atlantic No 39 was named *La France* in June 1913 for a special run in conjunction with the second visit of the French President, M Raymond Poincaré, from Portsmouth to Victoria, and retained the name until renamed *Hartland Point* in January 1926 *M. Joly Collection*

Below: The second batch of Atlantics appeared during Lawson Billinton's superintendency. Here 'H2' No 421 painted slate grey has been photographed at East Croydon between 1911 and 1913. Note the brakes originally fitted to the bogie, and the Company monogram appearing on each splasher. *J. R. Minnis Collection*

Above: No 326 *Bessborough* designed by Marsh but completed by Billinton in repose at Redhill in 1924. It seems a pity that together with *Abergavenny* these two were the only locomotives of their type to be built for they were highly successful performers.
O. J. Morris/Lens of Sutton

Centre left: One of the very modern looking 'E2' tanks No 104 photographed most unusually on a passenger train. The date is 1926, during the coal strike when Nos 103/4/6 and 7 were used on Crystal Palace services. The train comprising a mixed array of R. Billinton stock is entering Honor Oak Park station.
O. J. Morris

Bottom left: No 330 at Brighton. The last five Baltics only appeared after the war, No 330 entering service in December 1921. Its immaculate condition would indicate that the photograph was taken soon afterwards. *Lens of Sutton*

Above left: No 331 looking suitably massive as it leaves Victoria with a most interesting train. The profiles of the leading four carriages vary to a considerable degree. The first two are ex-South London electric 1sts converted for main line use in 1912 and still retaining bars across the droplights, followed by an arc roofed carriage and then a semi elliptical.
F. E. Mackay/IAL

Bottom left: Glinting in the evening sun, 'L' class No 332 passes the mound at Patcham with a northbound train. The rolling stock is again very mixed. Leading is 3rd class Pullman car No 3 formerly *Alexandra* of 1897, the semi-elliptical brake 3rd and lavatory composite, three American type Pullmans.
H. Gordon Tidey/Real Photographs

Above: 'K' class No 337 at Eastbourne. An example of the LBSCR's favourite location for official photographs where the expanse of grass and outline of the downs provided an attractive neutral background.
G. F. Burtt/LPC

Right: Possibly the finest known photograph of a 'K' class 2-6-0. No 344 in the surprisingly clean roundhouse at Battersea.
Rail Archive Stephenson

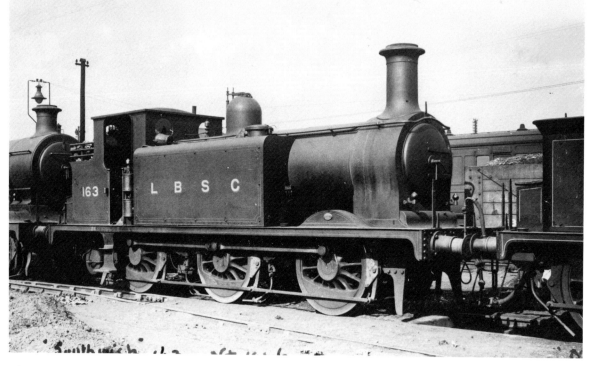

Above: In the last years of the LBSCR's existence many freight locomotives that had carried the lined black livery were repainted in the passenger umber. One such was 'E1' No 163, one of the six completed by Billinton and immediately distinguishable by the lack of combined splasher and sandbox seen here at New Cross in 1926. *O. J. Morris/Bluebell Archives*

Below: The Atlantics take over with a vengeance! At first glance this appears to be a double-headed train at Victoria. It is in fact an empty stock train to Eardley Road carriage sidings with 'H2' No 421 piloting No 425. 'H1' No 39 stands at the head of the train in the opposite platform. The date is 1924.
O. J. Morris/D. J. W. Brough Collection

Top: 'C3' No 303 on a Horsham-Bognor goods near Arundel in 1925. One of the ubiquitous Stroudley brakes leads. *O. J. Morris/D. J. W. Brough Collection*

Above: The final design to appear from Brighton Works before the Grouping was the 'B4' rebuild, classified as 'B4X'. Only the first carried LBSCR on its tender. In 1926, No 71 hauls a train consisting of carriages from the royal train near Honor Oak Park. *O. J. Morris/IAL*

Top right: 'D1' No 273 about to be lifted by the Brighton steam crane after being derailed at Eridge on 5 April 1916 while hauling the 8.00 Tunbridge Wells-Brighton. Some soldiers appear to be taking a hand on the right. Behind them are the two Stroudley brake 3rds of the breakdown train. *K. Marx Collection*

Centre right: Streatham Common shunting box after being hit during an air raid on the night of 23/24 September 1916. The box which dated from 1903 was rebuilt and survived until 1973.
M. Joly Collection

Below: One result of World War 1 was that women replaced many railwaymen away serving with the forces. Many acted as booking clerks but Rowfant was possibly unique in having a station mistress seen here at her station in 1921. Rowfant had a delightful building with small diamond paned windows which was erected in 1855 to serve Rowfant House. The original owner of that mansion, Commander Locker Lampson, who had given land for the railway, stipulated that an alcove, seen behind the nameboard, be provided with stone seats to provide shelter for his coachman who met him with his trap on his return by rail from the metropolis. It was situated deep in the forest and was one of the most remote stations on the system. The nameboard is of the standard pattern with cut out wooden letters that superseded the earlier painted variety c1900. On the right the covered stairs provides one of the few glimpses of the station footbridge. *Bluebell Archives*

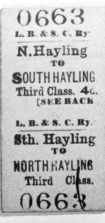

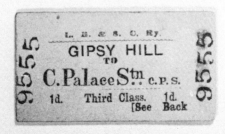
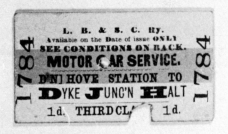

Above and overleaf: Brighton tickets were of sufficient variety to make their collection an interesting sideline of the railway hobby. Characteristic of the majority of standard types was the initialled repetition of the station destination to facilitate recognition.

First class were white, second blue and third drab, though these colours came in various shades with the printing spanning more than half a century. The ticket to Chelsea over the WLER is green, while the Perambulator and the Monday excursion ticket are shades of the same colour. The return tickets were striped in yellow or more latterly red, the colour generally used for diagonal or horizontal bands on single tickets. The motor car tickets were yellow separated by a rose band, and the later platform tickets consisted of the famous 'red blob' which was prolonged well into the Southern regime.

The selection of examples include several from long closed branch lines like the Kemp Town and Hayling Island, from stations whose names have since been changed or adapted like New Brighton (Hove), New Croydon (East Croydon), Old Kent Road and Hatcham; one rare example of 1891 from the erstwhile platform at Grosvenor Road where incoming tickets were collected, and three examples of joint railway tickets with the Brighton's two big neighbours. The majority of the above examples are of the 1890s and the latest example, the Worthing Rail Motor, dates from 1915.
K. Marx Collection

9481 — L. B. & S. C. RY.
TICKET FOR PERAMBULATOR OR MAIL CART.
When accompanied by passenger.
EAST CROYDON TO
Victoria.v.
RATE 6d.
At Passenger's Risk. For conditions see back hereof This Ticket must be given up on arrival. — 9481

4434 — L. B. & S. C. RY.
LONDON BRIDGE
CHILD
EASTBOURNE ea
via LEWES.
2s. 4d. THIRD CLASS. 2s. 4d. — 4434

0556 — L. B. & S. C. Ry.
VICTORIA
To
Grosvenor Rd. Grd.
1½d. SECOND CLASS. 1½d.
Grosvenor Rd. [See Back. — 0556

9247 — L. B. & S. C. & S. E. & C. RYS.
Available on the DATE of issue ONLY.
This ticket is issued subject to the Regulations & Conditions stated in the Joint Companies Time Tables & Bills.
OXTED
TO
UPPER WARLINGHAM u.w.
5d. THIRD CLASS. 5d. — 9247

0177 — L. B. & S. C. Ry
Available on the DATE of issue ONLY
SEE CONDITIONS AT BACK.
BALHAM
TO
CLAPHAM JN. c.j.
7d. First Cl. 7d. — 0177

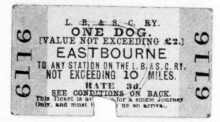

3391 — L. B. & S. C. Ry.
KENSINGTON
TO
Chelsea.ch
Third Class. 2d.
Chelsea [See Back. — 3391

6988 — L. B. & S. C. Ry.
KEMP TOWN
No 2] TO
LEWES R'D l.r.
1d. THIRD CLASS. 1d.
[See Back — 16988

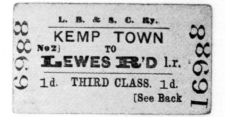

6116 — L. B. & S. C. RY.
ONE DOG.
[VALUE NOT EXCEEDING £2.]
EASTBOURNE
TO ANY STATION ON THE L. B. & S. C. RY.
NOT EXCEEDING 10 MILES.
RATE 3d.
SEE CONDITIONS ON BACK.
This Ticket is available for a single journey Only, and must be given up on arrival. — 6116

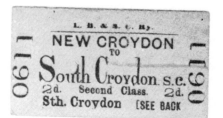

4816 — L. B. & S. C. Ry.
BRIGHTON
No 1] TO
West Brighton
1½d. THIRD CLASS. 1½d.
[See Back — 4816

0079 — L. B. & S. C. RY.
Issued subject to conditions in Co's Time Tables
VICTORIA
Local] TO [Local
WANDSWORTH O.
Available on the
MONDAY
in the week ending
JUNE 5th 1909.
THIRD CLASS.

L. B. & S. C. RY.
Issued subject to conditions in Co's Time Tables
WANDSWORTH COM
Local] TO [Local
VICTORIA
Available on the
MONDAY
in the week ending
JUNE 5th. 1909.
THIRD CLASS. — 0079

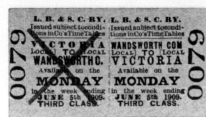

0190 — L. B. & S. C. Ry.
NEW CROYDON
TO
South Croydon s.c.
2d. Second Class. 2d.
Sth. Croydon [SEE BACK — 0190

59560 — 1 | 2 | 3 | 4 | 5 | 6
LONDON BRIGHTON & SOUTH COAST RAILWAY.
LEWES
Admit ONE to Platform Charge ½d
This ticket must be given up on leaving Platform
Available ONE HOUR. For conditions see back
7 | 8 | 9 | 10 | 11 | 12 — 59560

Above: An array of Brighton lamps. There are three signal lamps pictured of which the smallest is for a ground signal. Of the two headlamps, the one with the slim wire type handle is the older, dating from 1882. The tail lamp is of the later type, and the lamp with the glass chimney is the interior of a platform lantern. *S. D. Everest/R. F. Resch Collection*

Left: A selection of badges and buttons. The badges from top left: Station Master (gilt), Passenger Guard (silver), Porter (silver), also used by SR; First Aider (silver) worn on sleeve. The shoulder badges shown are of the earlier and later pattern, also the Fratton and East Southsea Joint Line (all silver). Buttons depicted from left to right: Higher grades ie station master, inspector etc (gilt — featuring coat of arms), other ranks (silver) great coat, jacket, waistcoat; Croydon and Oxted joint C&OR (brass); LB&SCRy Steam Packets (gilt). *S. D. Everest/R. F. Resch Collection*

Above: 'E4' No 580 running as 2-4-2T on mixed train,
photographed between 1906 and 1909.
M. Joly Collection

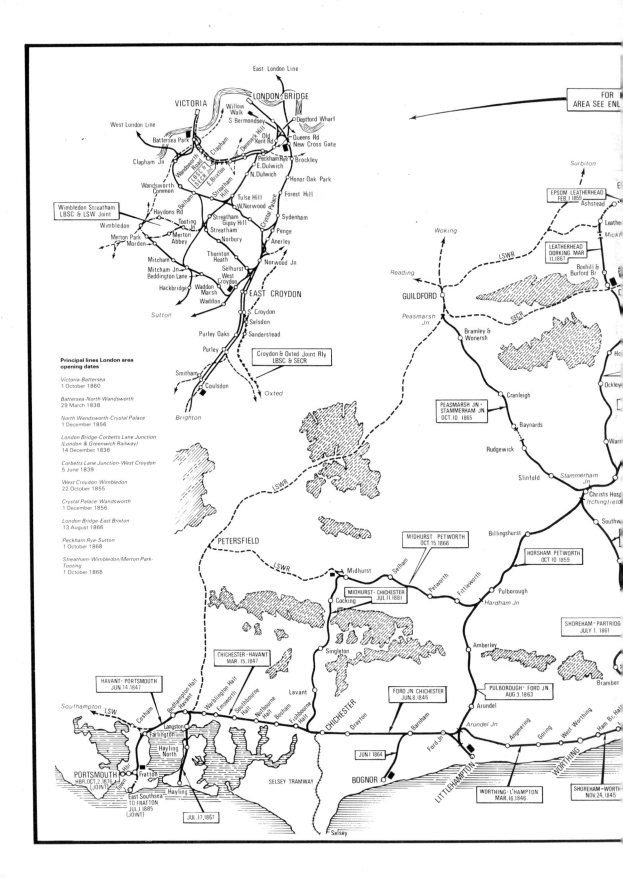

Principal lines London area opening dates

Victoria-Battersea
1 October 1860

Battersea-North Wandsworth
29 March 1838

North Wandsworth-Crystal Palace
1 December 1856

London Bridge-Corbetts Lane Junction
(London & Greenwich Railway)
14 December 1836

Corbetts Lane Junction-West Croydon
5 June 1839

West Croydon-Wimbledon
22 October 1855

Crystal Palace-Wandsworth
1 December 1856

London Bridge-East Brixton
13 August 1866

Peckham Rye-Sutton
1 October 1868

Streatham-Wimbledon/Merton Park-
Tooting
1 October 1868